Taking Your Pet to the Vet

CANADIAN CATALOGUING IN PUBLICATION DATA
David Seidman
Taking your pet to the vet : cartoons

ISBN 1-55022-429-8

1. Pet medicine — Caricatures and cartoons. I. Seidman, David, 1958 June 8– .

NC1763.P42T34 2000   741.5´9   C00-931712-0

Cover and interior design by Tania Craan
Layout by Mary Bowness
Printed by Transcontinental

Distributed in Canada by General Distribution Services, 325 Humber College Blvd., Toronto, Ontario M9W 7C3
Distributed in the United States by LPC Group, 1436 West Randolph Street, Chicago, Illinois, U.S.A. 60607

Published by ECW PRESS
2120 Queen Street East, Suite 200,
Toronto, Ontario, M4E 1E2
ecwpress.com

PRINTED AND BOUND IN CANADA

Taking Your Pet to the Vet

cartoons collected by David Seidman

ECW PRESS

Dedication

To the staff of the Los Angeles Times Syndicate, 1982-1988, especially Annie Banks, Cathy Mestas, and Lee Nording, who rescued a young comics editor when he needed rescuing and helped him make sense out of the crazy business of cartoons.

Acknowledgments

I would like to acknowledge the help of the following people in preparing this book: Bill Blackbeard, Mary Bowness, Daryl Cagle (who doesn't even know what he did), Tania Craan, Jack David, Paul Levine, Rick Marschall, Tracey Millen, and Robert Pinnock.

— David Seidman

Table of Contents

Take Me to Your Vet

Garfield ®
by Jim Davis
I'M GOING TO TAKE YOU TO THE VET FOR A CHECKUP, GARFIELD
OH-NO!
6-25
MY UNCLE BARNEY WENT TO THE VET ONCE
HE CAME BACK AS MY AUNT BERNICE
JIM DAVIS

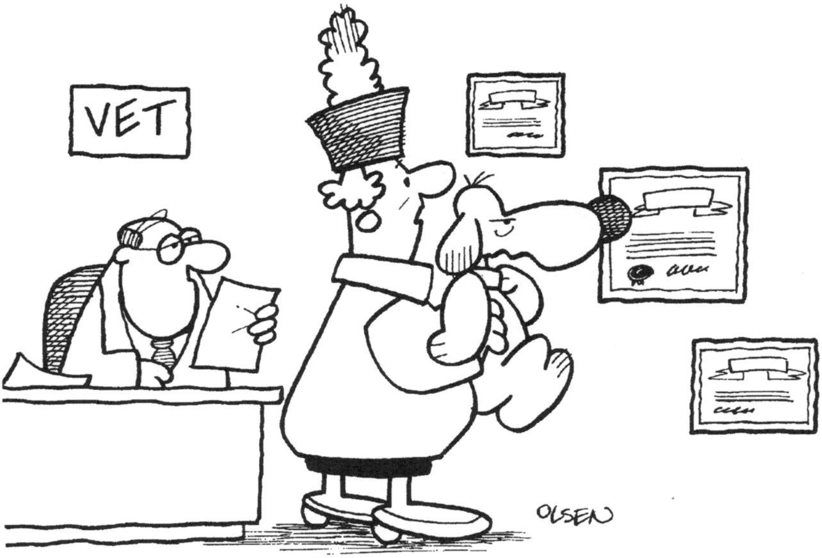
VET
OLSEN

- WELL, BELLA - CONVINCED !?

Mother Goose & Grimm

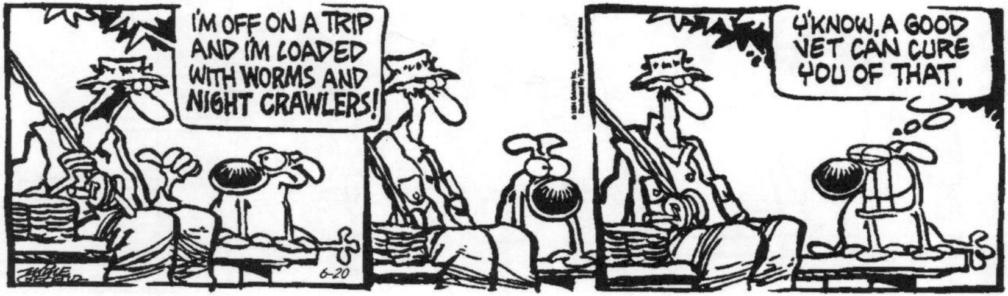
I'M OFF ON A TRIP AND I'M LOADED WITH WORMS AND NIGHT CRAWLERS!
Y'KNOW, A GOOD VET CAN CURE YOU OF THAT.
6-20

Mutts

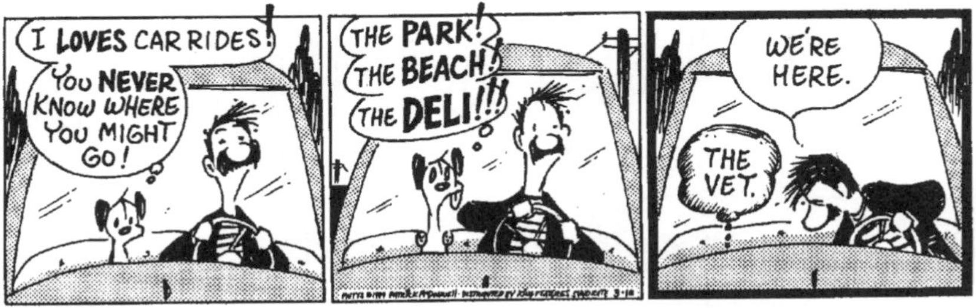
I **LOVES** CAR RIDES!
YOU **NEVER** KNOW WHERE YOU MIGHT GO!
THE PARK!
THE BEACH!
THE **DELI**!!!
WE'RE HERE.
THE VET.

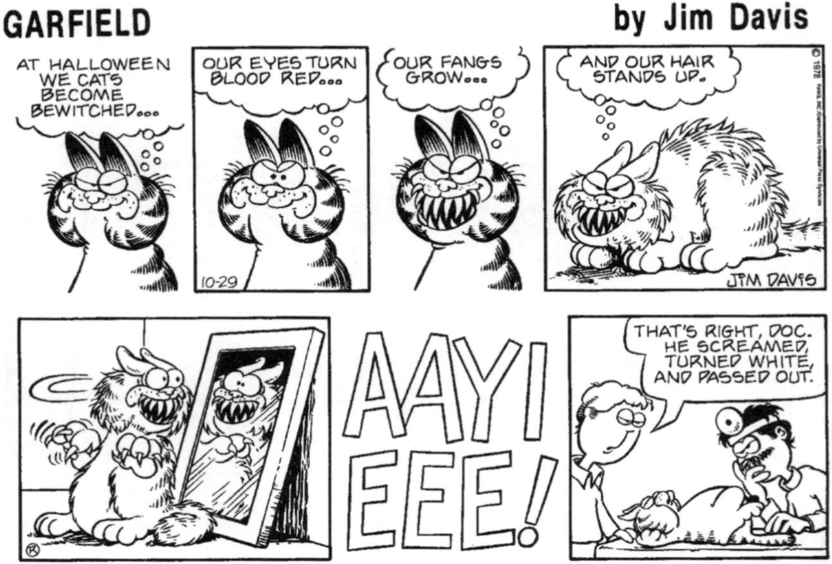
GARFIELD
by Jim Davis
AT HALLOWEEN WE CATS BECOME BEWITCHED...
OUR EYES TURN BLOOD RED...
10-29
OUR FANGS GROW...
AND OUR HAIR STANDS UP.
JIM DAVIS
AAYIEEE!
THAT'S RIGHT, DOC. HE SCREAMED, TURNED WHITE, AND PASSED OUT.

Mother Goose & Grimm

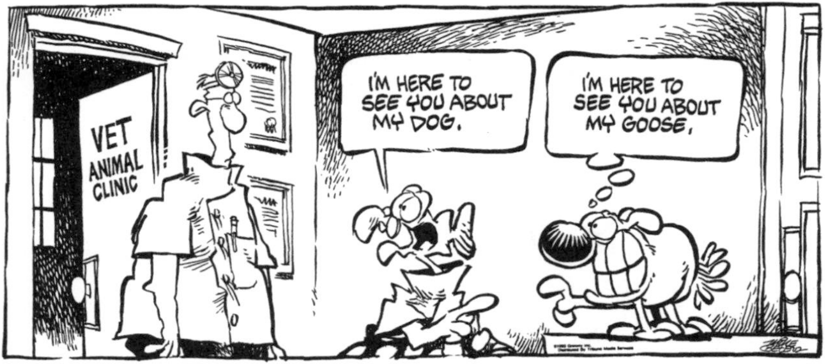
VET
ANIMAL
CLINIC
I'M HERE TO SEE YOU ABOUT MY DOG.
I'M HERE TO SEE YOU ABOUT MY GOOSE.

Robotman

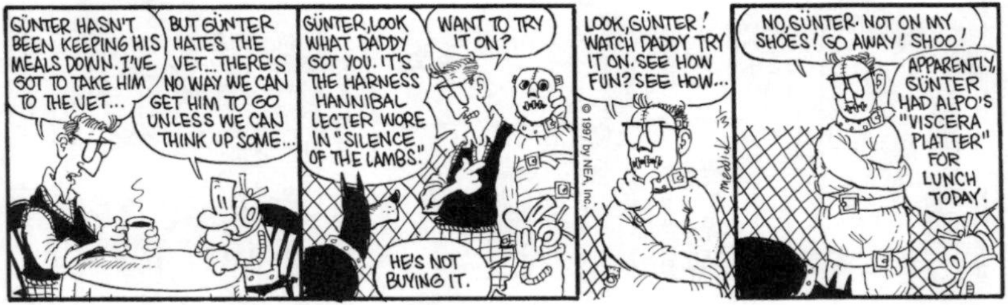
GÜNTER HASN'T BEEN KEEPING HIS MEALS DOWN. I'VE GOT TO TAKE HIM TO THE VET...
BUT GÜNTER HATES THE VET... THERE'S NO WAY WE CAN GET HIM TO GO UNLESS WE CAN THINK UP SOME...
GÜNTER, LOOK WHAT DADDY GOT YOU. IT'S THE HARNESS HANNIBAL LECTER WORE IN "SILENCE OF THE LAMBS."
WANT TO TRY IT ON?
HE'S NOT BUYING IT.
LOOK, GÜNTER! WATCH DADDY TRY IT ON. SEE HOW FUN? SEE HOW...
© 1997 by NEA, Inc.
meddick 1/13
NO, GÜNTER. NOT ON MY SHOES! GO AWAY! SHOO!
APPARENTLY, GÜNTER HAD ALPO'S "VISCERA PLATTER" FOR LUNCH TODAY.

Robotman

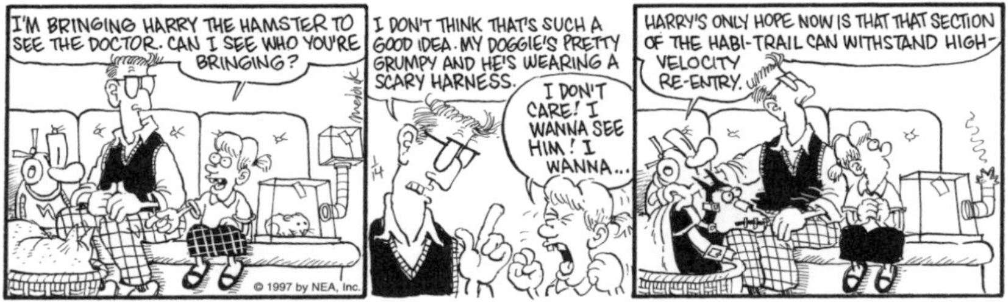
I'M BRINGING HARRY THE HAMSTER TO SEE THE DOCTOR. CAN I SEE WHO YOU'RE BRINGING?
© 1997 by NEA, Inc.
I DON'T THINK THAT'S SUCH A GOOD IDEA. MY DOGGIE'S PRETTY GRUMPY AND HE'S WEARING A SCARY HARNESS.
I DON'T CARE! I WANNA SEE HIM! I WANNA...
HARRY'S ONLY HOPE NOW IS THAT THAT SECTION OF THE HABI-TRAIL CAN WITHSTAND HIGH-VELOCITY RE-ENTRY.

Robotman

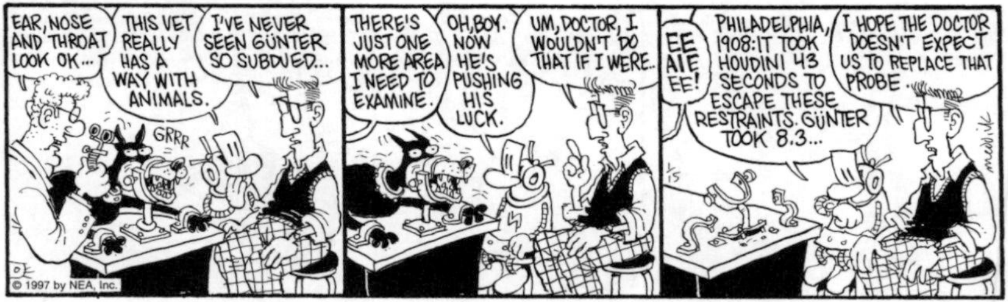

EAR, NOSE AND THROAT LOOK OK...
THIS VET REALLY HAS A WAY WITH ANIMALS.
I'VE NEVER SEEN GÜNTER SO SUBDUED...
GRRR
THERE'S JUST ONE MORE AREA I NEED TO EXAMINE.
OH, BOY. NOW HE'S PUSHING HIS LUCK.
UM, DOCTOR, I WOULDN'T DO THAT IF I WERE..
EE AIE EE!
PHILADELPHIA, 1908: IT TOOK HOUDINI 43 SECONDS TO ESCAPE THESE RESTRAINTS. GÜNTER TOOK 8.3...
I HOPE THE DOCTOR DOESN'T EXPECT US TO REPLACE THAT PROBE.

Reality Check

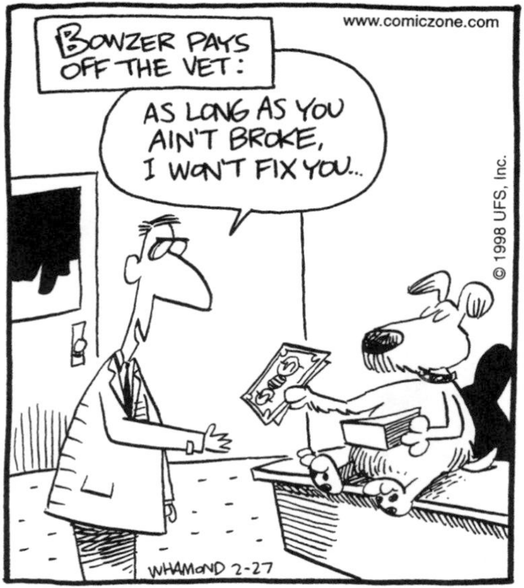
www.comiczone.com
BOWZER PAYS OFF THE VET:
AS LONG AS YOU AIN'T BROKE, I WON'T FIX YOU...
© 1998 UFS, Inc.
WHAMOND 2-27

DOWNES
USA

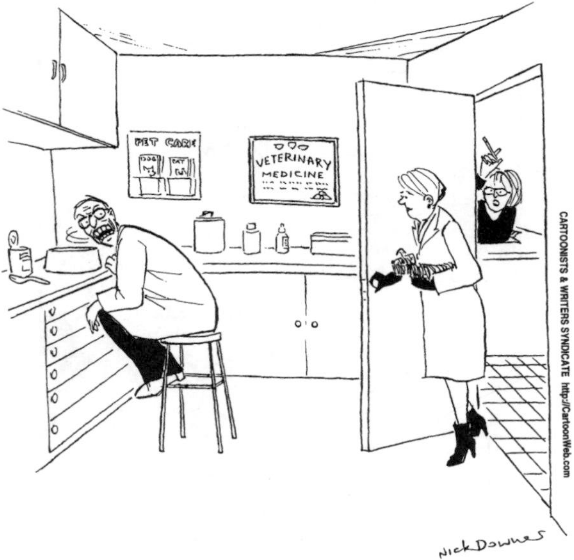
PET CARE
DOG
CAT
VETERINARY
MEDICINE
Nick Downes

"Oh, Ma'am–I wouldn't bother him while he's eating!"

Waiting Room

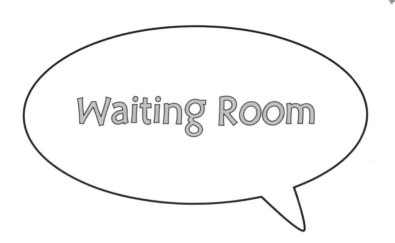

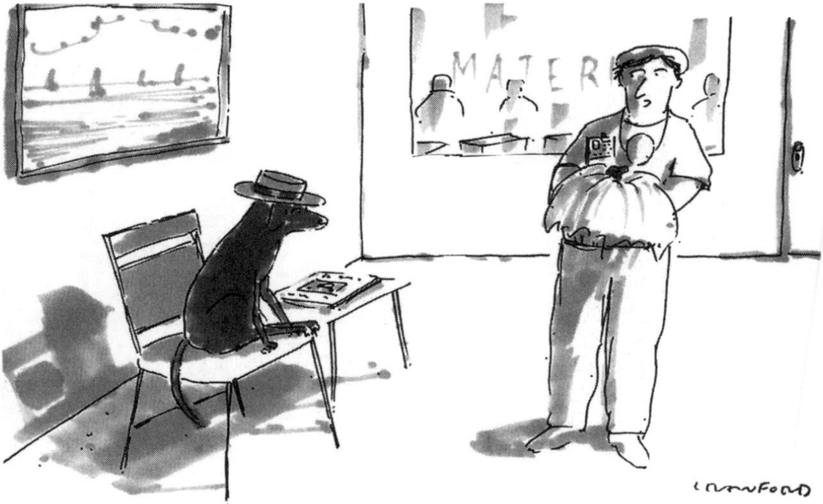
MATER

"Congratulations! It's a bitch!"

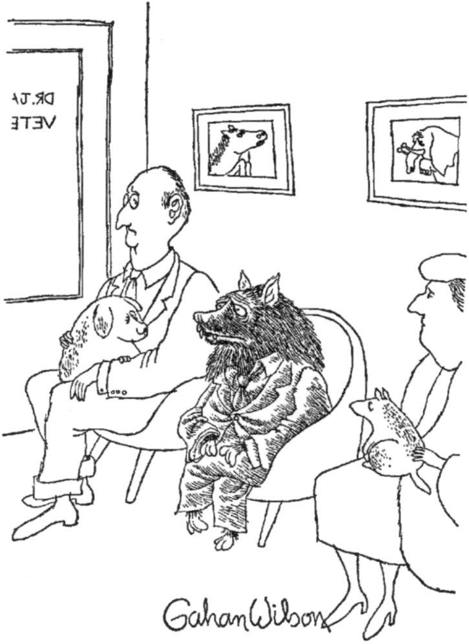
Gahan Wilson

CITIZEN DOG **BY MARK O'HARE**

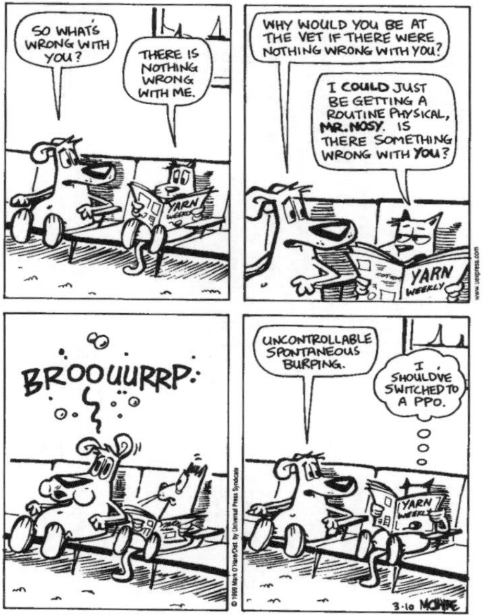

SO WHAT'S WRONG WITH YOU?
THERE IS NOTHING WRONG WITH ME.
YARN WEEKLY
WHY WOULD YOU BE AT THE VET IF THERE WERE NOTHING WRONG WITH YOU?
I COULD JUST BE GETTING A ROUTINE PHYSICAL, MR. NOSY. IS THERE SOMETHING WRONG WITH YOU?
YARN WEEKLY
www.uexpress.com
BROOUURRP
© 1999 Mark O'Hare/Dist. by Universal Press Syndicate
UNCONTROLLABLE SPONTANEOUS BURPING.
I SHOULD'VE SWITCHED TO A PPO.
YARN WEEKLY
3-10 M'OHARE

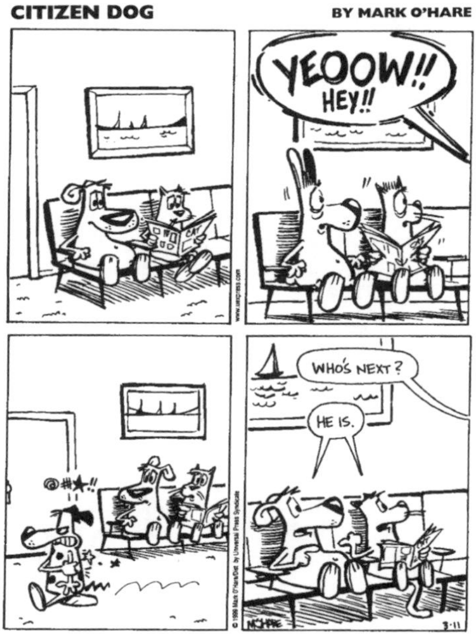
CITIZEN DOG
BY MARK O'HARE
YEOOW!!
HEY!!
@#★!!
WHO'S NEXT?
HE IS.
© 1999 Mark O'Hare/Dist. by Universal Press Syndicate
3-11

Cornered by Baldwin

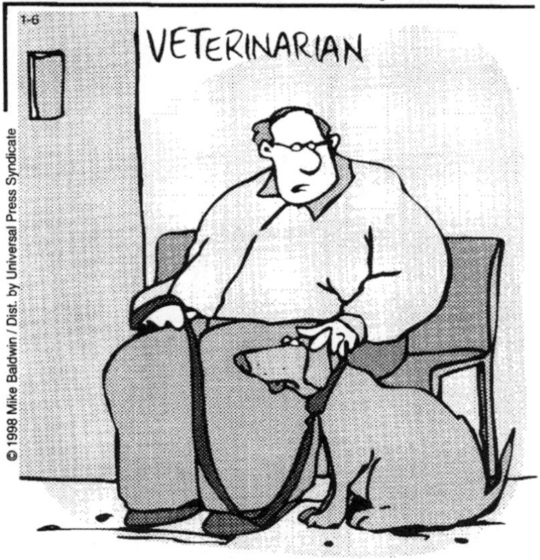
1-6
VETERINARIAN
© 1998 Mike Baldwin / Dist. by Universal Press Syndicate

"Just relax and let me do the talking."

GARFIELD by Jim Davis

VETERINARY CLINIC
HERE, PETEY. HERE, PETEY. WHERE ARE YOU ?
11-3
VETERINARY CLINIC
BURP!
JIM DAVIS

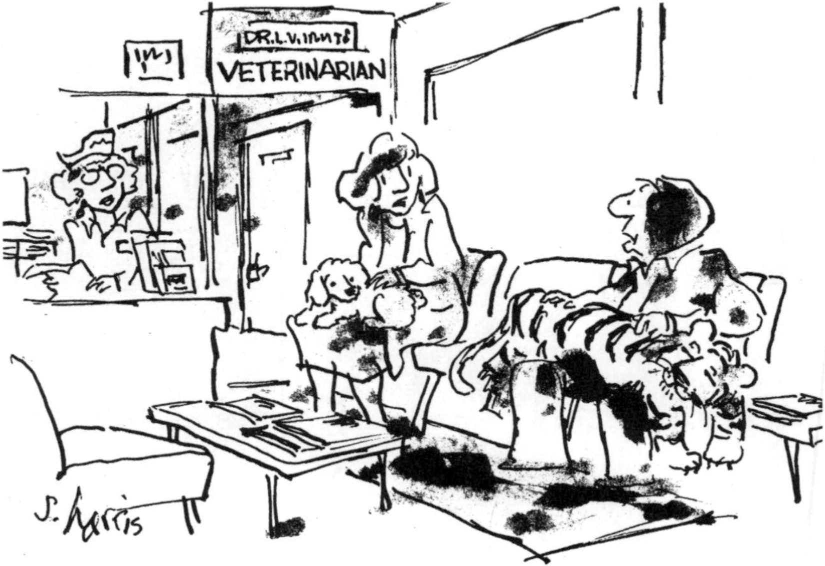
VETERINARIAN
S. Harris

"COULD WE GO IN AHEAD OF YOU? HIS TRANQUILIZER IS WEARING OFF."

Examination Room

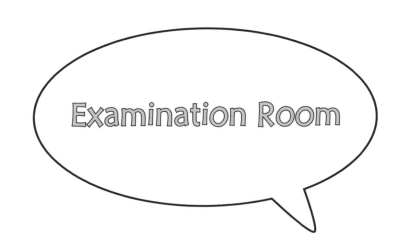

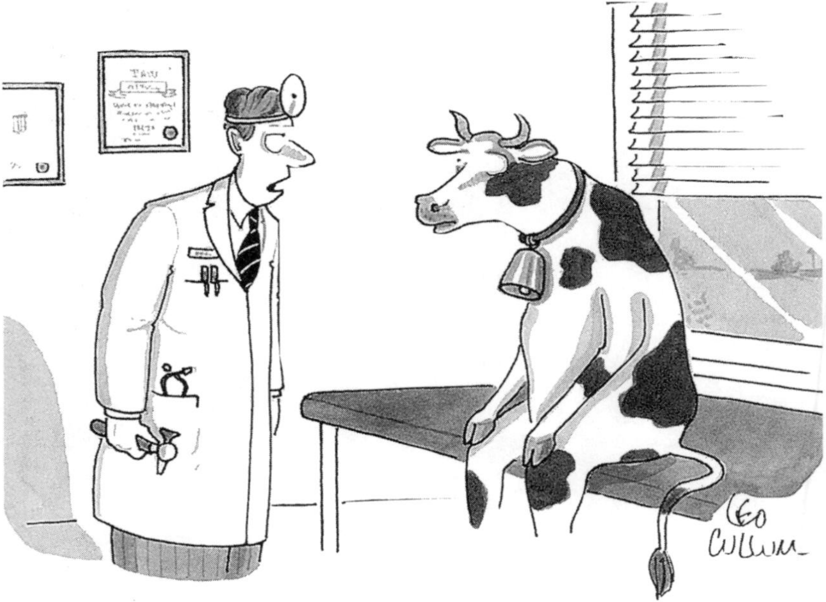

"The ringing in your ears — I think I can help."

Mother Goose & Grimm

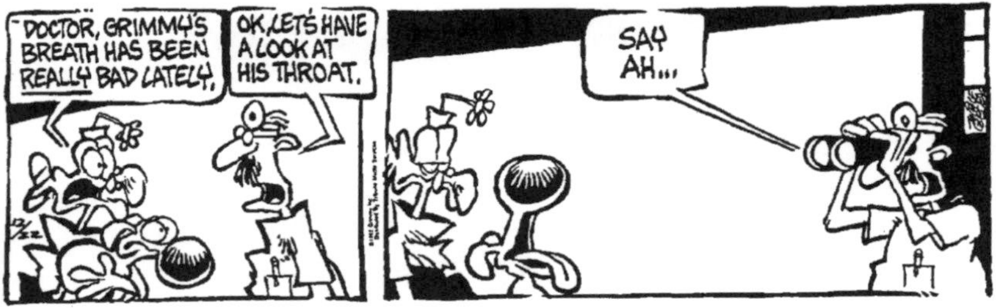
DOCTOR, GRIMMY'S BREATH HAS BEEN REALLY BAD LATELY.
OK, LET'S HAVE A LOOK AT HIS THROAT.
SAY AH...

CITIZEN DOG

BY MARK O'HARE

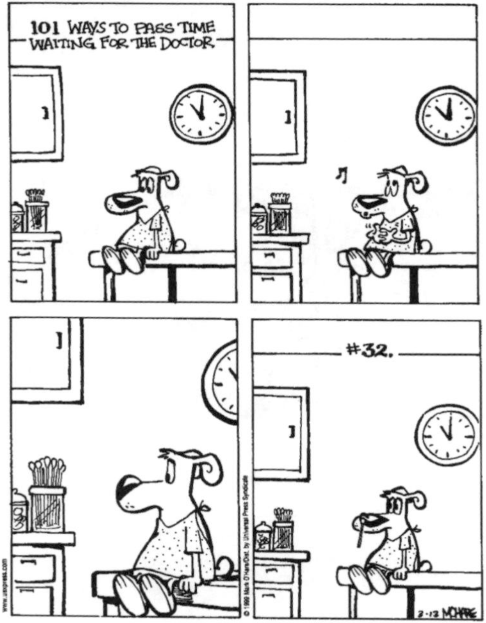

101 WAYS TO PASS TIME WAITING FOR THE DOCTOR
#32.
3-13 M.O'HARE

Garfield ®
by Jim Davis
SAY, "AH," GARFIELD
2-1
I'LL TAKE YOUR TEMPERATURE IF YOU DON'T SAY, "AH"
PAWS, INC./Distributed by Universal Press Syndicate
AH
JIM DAVIS
© 1980 United Feature Syndicate, Inc.

off the mark by Mark Parisi

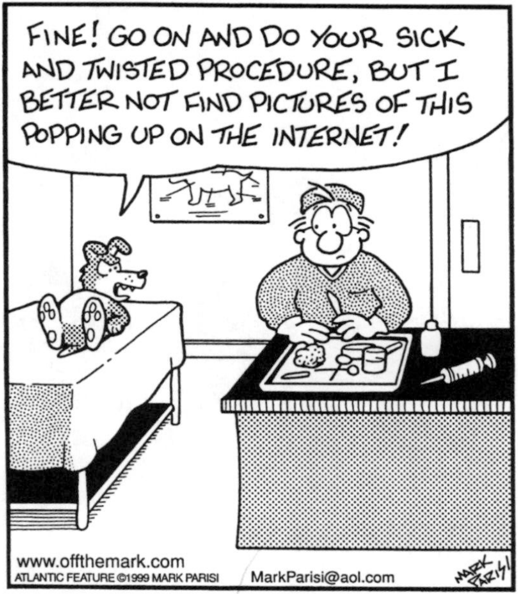
FINE! GO ON AND DO YOUR SICK AND TWISTED PROCEDURE, BUT I BETTER NOT FIND PICTURES OF THIS POPPING UP ON THE INTERNET!
www.offthemark.com
ATLANTIC FEATURE ©1999 MARK PARISI
MarkParisi@aol.com
MARK PARISI

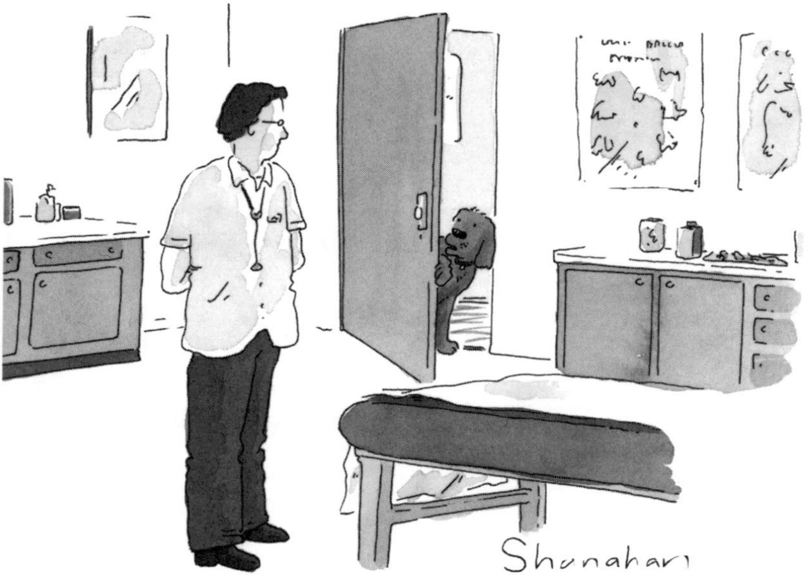
Shanahan

"I seem to have missed the cup."

Mother Goose & Grimm

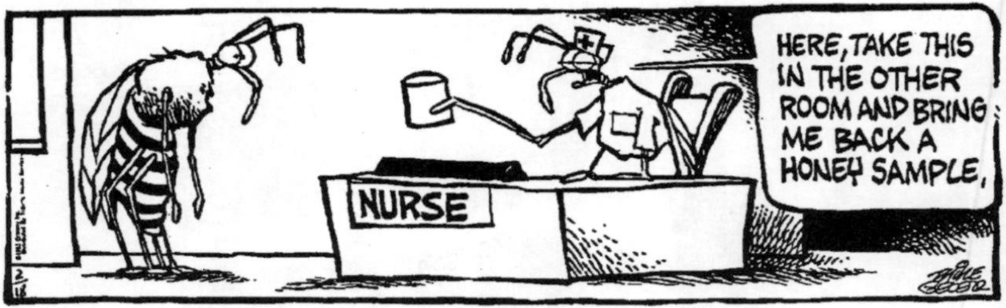
NURSE
HERE, TAKE THIS IN THE OTHER ROOM AND BRING ME BACK A HONEY SAMPLE,

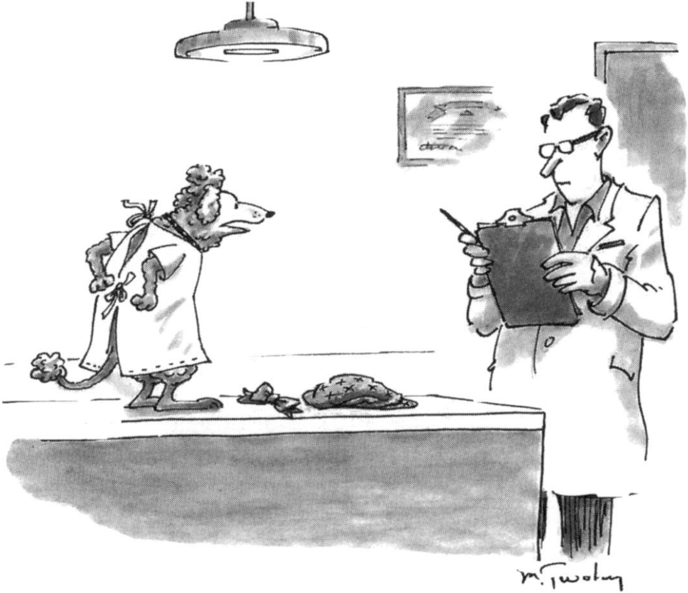

"May I keep my collar on?"

HERMAN®

by Jim Unger

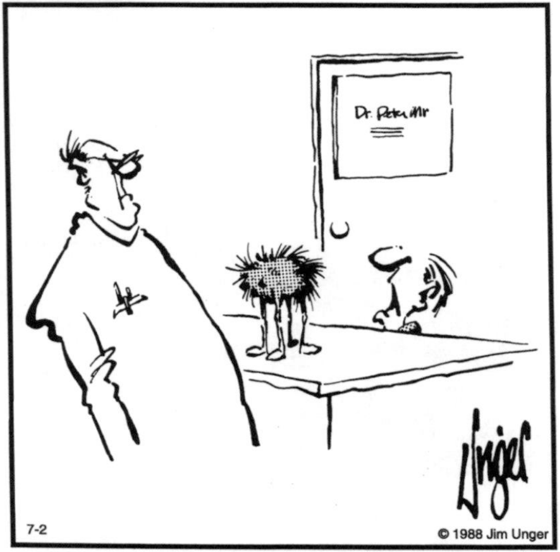
7-2
© 1988 Jim Unger

“*You’re* a vet. Don’t *you* know what it is?”

CITIZEN DOG
BY MARK O'HARE
CHANGING ROOM
I ALWAYS GET EMBARRASSED WEARING A PATIENT GOWN.
4
AND I'M A DOG. I DON'T EVEN **WEAR** CLOTHES.
3-12 MO'HARE

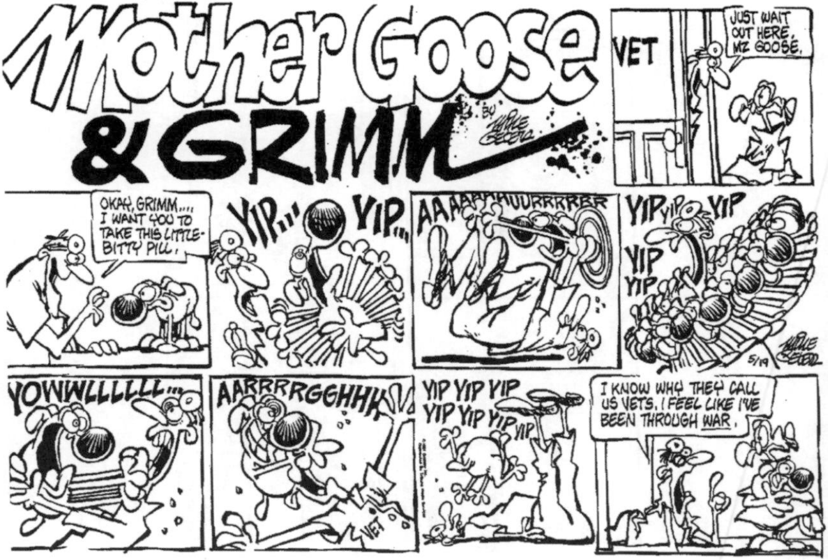
Mother Goose
& GRIMM
BY
VET
JUST WAIT OUT HERE, MZ GOOSE.
OKAY, GRIMM.... I WANT YOU TO TAKE THIS LITTLE-BITTY PILL.
YIP... YIP...
YIP YIP YIP
YIP YIP
YOWWLLLLLL...
AARRRRGGHHH
VET
YIP YIP YIP
YIP YIP YIP YIP
I KNOW WHY THEY CALL US VETS. I FEEL LIKE I'VE BEEN THROUGH WAR.

Say Meow

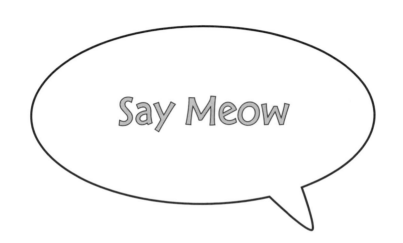

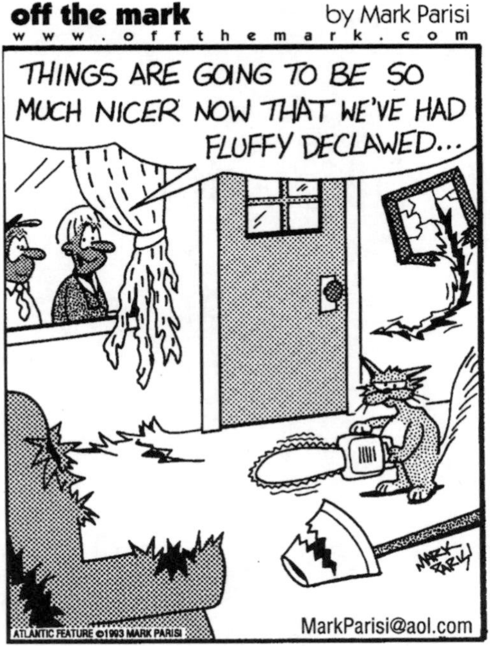
off the mark
by Mark Parisi
www.offthemark.com
THINGS ARE GOING TO BE SO MUCH NICER NOW THAT WE'VE HAD FLUFFY DECLAWED...
ATLANTIC FEATURE ©1993 MARK PARISI
MarkParisi@aol.com

Sylvia

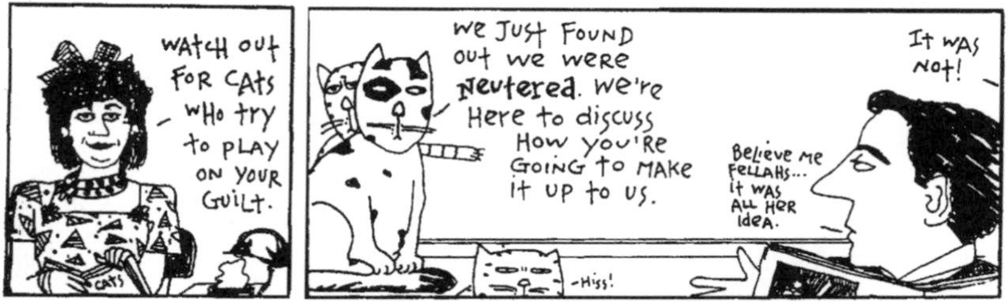
WATCH OUT FOR CATS WHO TRY TO PLAY ON YOUR GUILT.
CATS
WE JUST FOUND OUT WE WERE NEUTERED. WE'RE HERE TO DISCUSS HOW YOU'RE GOING TO MAKE IT UP TO US.
-HISS!
BELIEVE ME FELLAHS... IT WAS ALL HER IDEA.
IT WAS NOT!

Mother Goose & Grimm

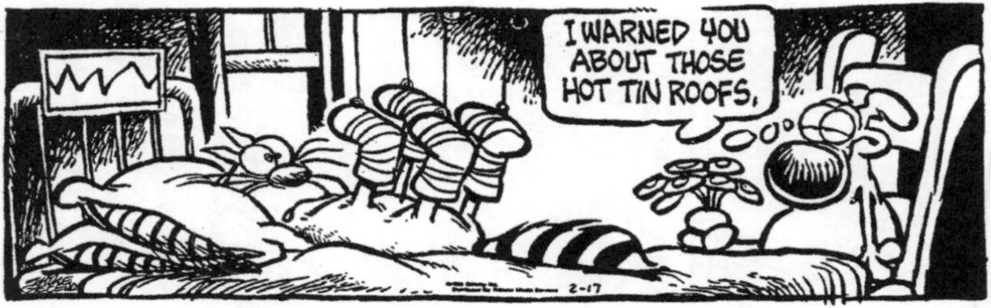
I WARNED YOU ABOUT THOSE HOT TIN ROOFS.
2-17

BIZARRO By DAN PIRARO

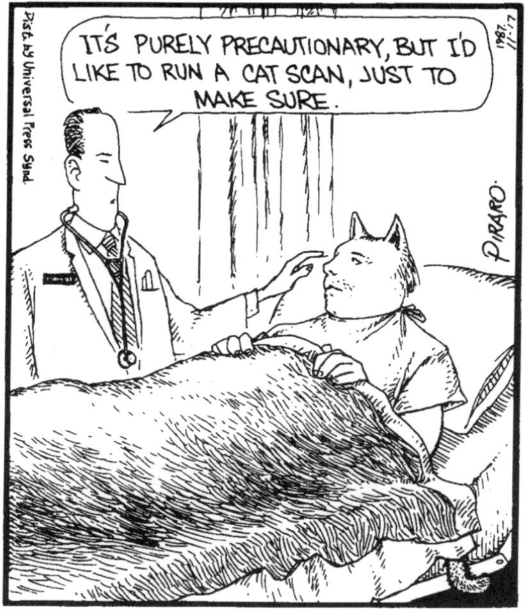
IT'S PURELY PRECAUTIONARY, BUT I'D LIKE TO RUN A CAT SCAN, JUST TO MAKE SURE.
Dist. by Universal Press Synd.
1987. 11-17
PIRARO

HEATHCLIFF

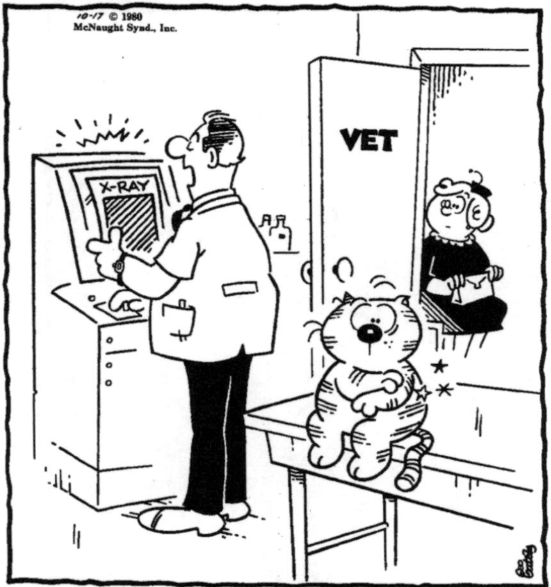
10-17 © 1980
McNaught Synd., Inc.
X-RAY
VET

" JUST AS I SUSPECTED... SCRATCHING POST ELBOW."

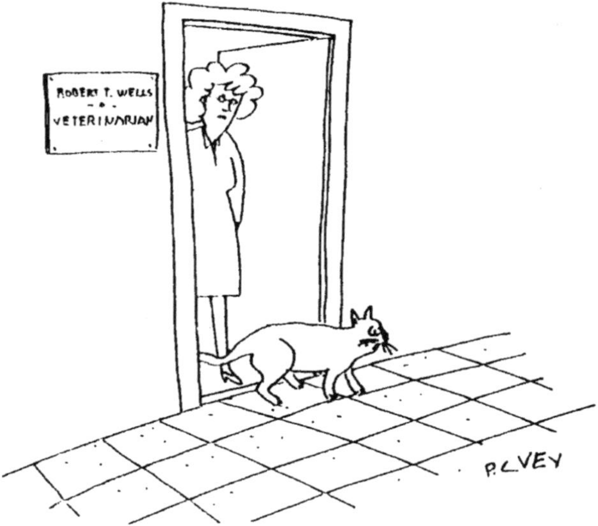
ROBERT T. WELLS
VETERINARIAN
P.C.VEY

"We don't care how cute you were as a kitten.
You still need an appointment to see the doctor."

Mother Goose & Grimm

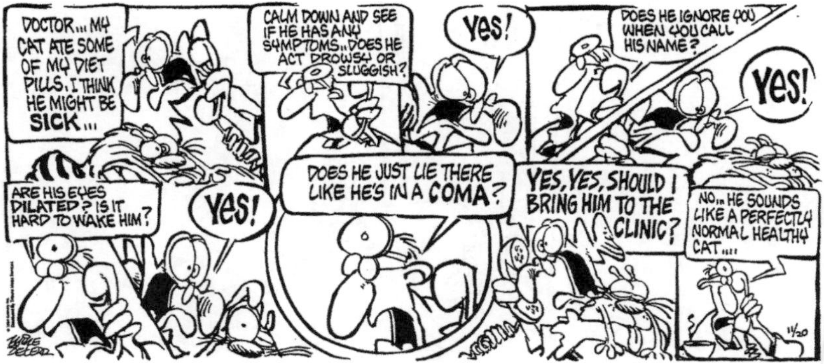
DOCTOR... MY CAT ATE SOME OF MY DIET PILLS. I THINK HE MIGHT BE SICK...
CALM DOWN AND SEE IF HE HAS ANY SYMPTOMS.. DOES HE ACT DROWSY OR SLUGGISH?
YES!
DOES HE IGNORE YOU WHEN YOU CALL HIS NAME?
YES!
ARE HIS EYES DILATED? IS IT HARD TO WAKE HIM?
YES!
DOES HE JUST LIE THERE LIKE HE'S IN A COMA?
YES, YES, SHOULD I BRING HIM TO THE CLINIC?
NO.. HE SOUNDS LIKE A PERFECTLY NORMAL HEALTHY CAT....
11/20

off the mark by Mark Parisi

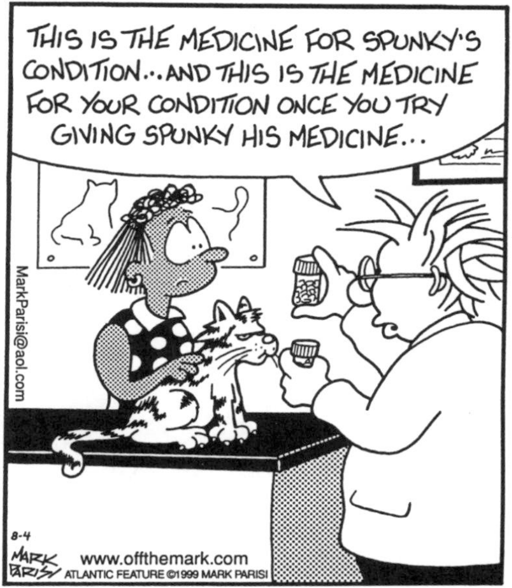
THIS IS THE MEDICINE FOR SPUNKY'S CONDITION...AND THIS IS THE MEDICINE FOR YOUR CONDITION ONCE YOU TRY GIVING SPUNKY HIS MEDICINE...
MarkParisi@aol.com
8-4
MARK PARISI
www.offthemark.com
ATLANTIC FEATURE ©1999 MARK PARISI

HEATHCLIFF

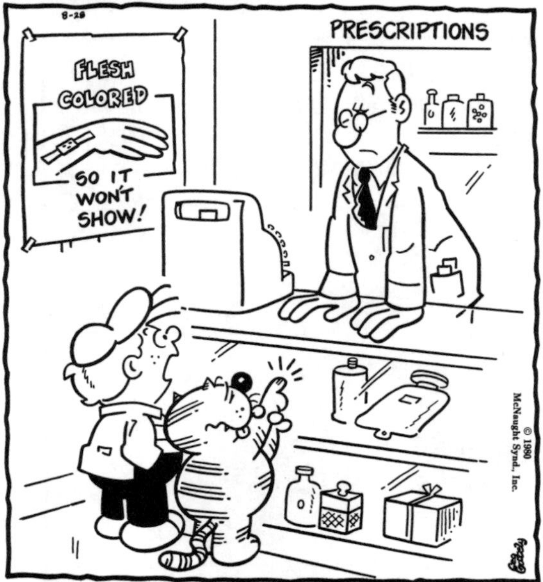
8-28
FLESH COLORED
SO IT WON'T SHOW!
PRESCRIPTIONS
© 1980 McNaught Synd., Inc.

"HAVE YOU GOT A TABBY COLORED BANDAID?"

HEATHCLIFF

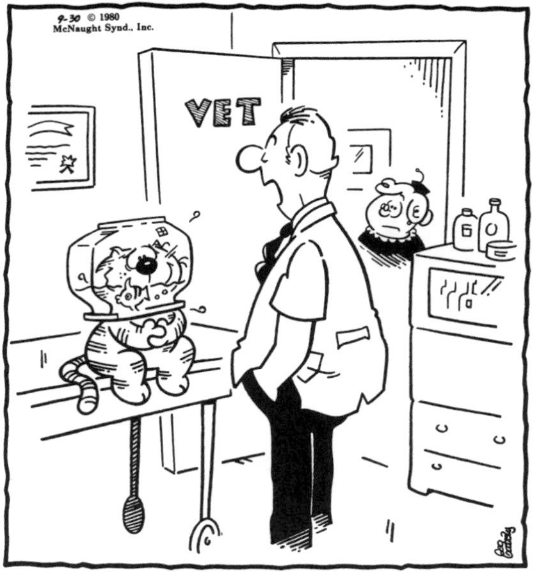

9-30 © 1980
McNaught Synd., Inc.
VET
G
O

"I THOUGHT I TOOK YOU OFF BETWEEN MEAL SNACKS ?!"

Rose Is Rose

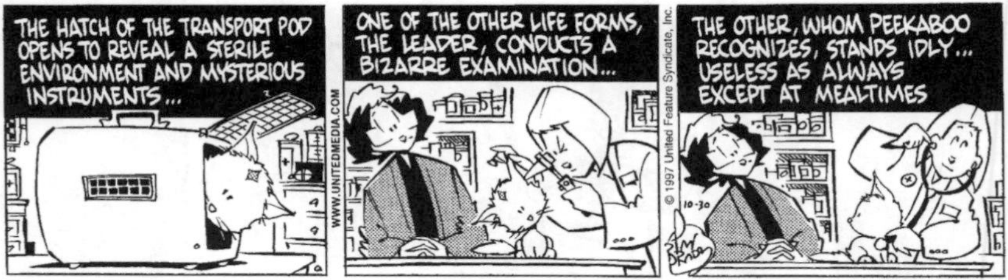
THE HATCH OF THE TRANSPORT POD OPENS TO REVEAL A STERILE ENVIRONMENT AND MYSTERIOUS INSTRUMENTS...
WWW.UNITEDMEDIA.COM
ONE OF THE OTHER LIFE FORMS, THE LEADER, CONDUCTS A BIZARRE EXAMINATION...
© 1997 United Feature Syndicate, Inc.
THE OTHER, WHOM PEEKABOO RECOGNIZES, STANDS IDLY... USELESS AS ALWAYS EXCEPT AT MEALTIMES
10-30

Sylvia

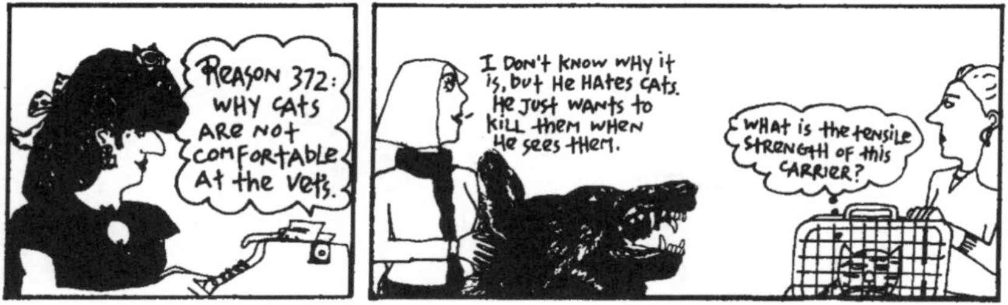
REASON 372: WHY CATS ARE NOT COMFORTABLE AT THE VET'S.
I DON'T KNOW WHY IT IS, BUT HE HATES CATS. HE JUST WANTS TO KILL THEM WHEN HE SEES THEM.
WHAT IS THE TENSILE STRENGTH OF THIS CARRIER?

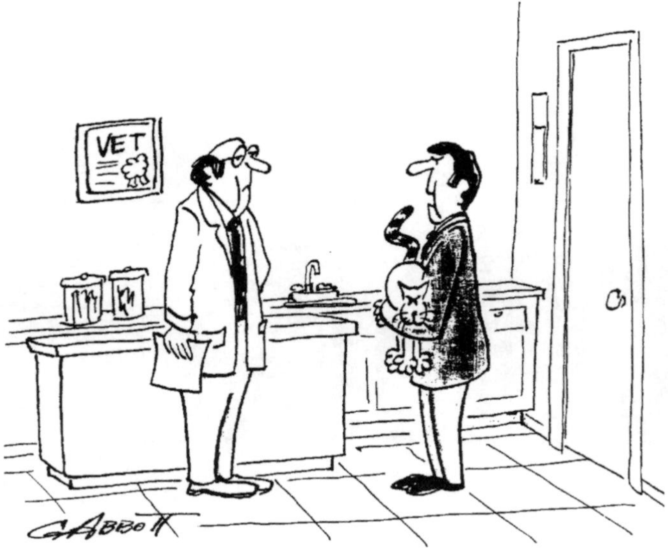
VET

"He's still ornery–can you fix something else?"

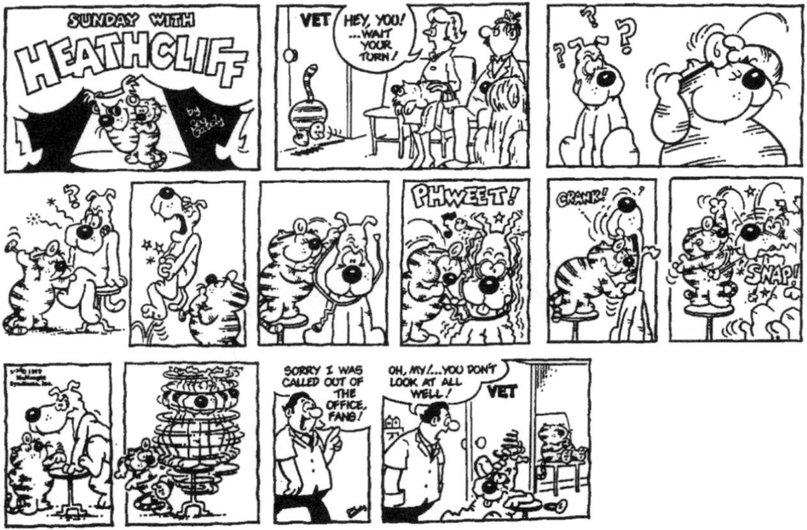
SUNDAY WITH
HEATHCLIFF
by
VET
HEY, YOU! ...WAIT YOUR TURN!
PHWEET!
CRANK!
SNAP!
SORRY I WAS CALLED OUT OF THE OFFICE, FANG!
OH, MY!...YOU DON'T LOOK AT ALL WELL!
VET

HEATHCLIFF

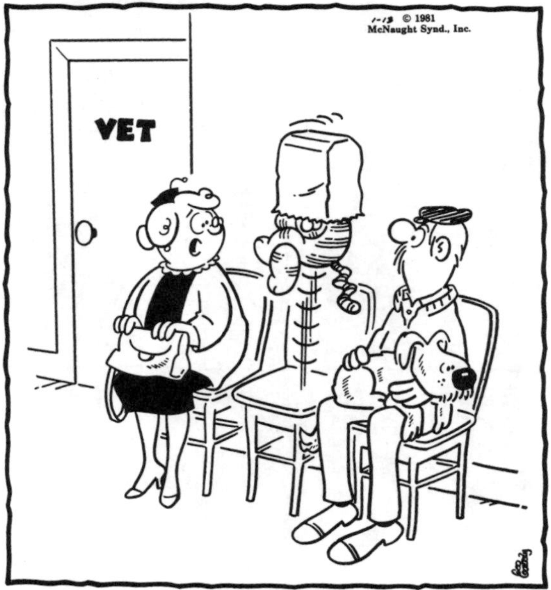
1-13 © 1981
McNaught Synd., Inc.
VET

"HICCUPS."

off the mark by Mark Parisi
www.offthemark.com

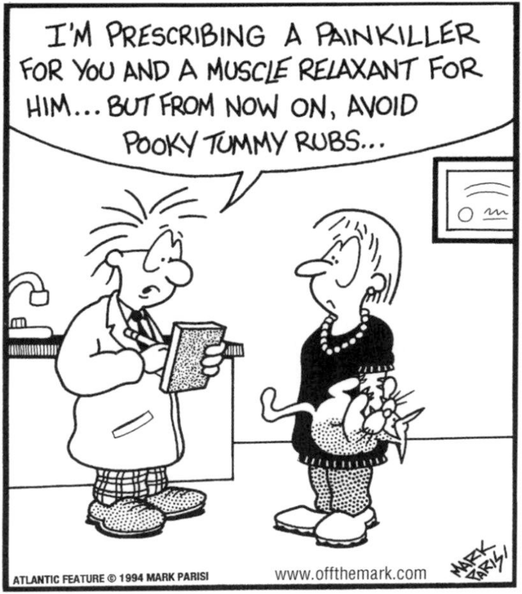

Mother Goose & Grimm

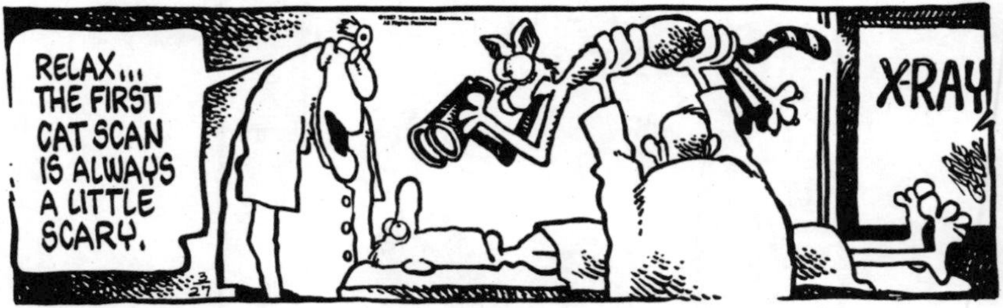
RELAX... THE FIRST CAT SCAN IS ALWAYS A LITTLE SCARY.
X-RAY

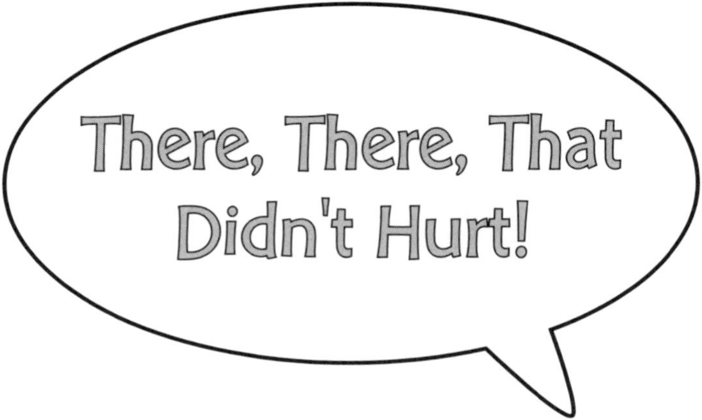
There, There, That Didn't Hurt!

HEATHCLIFF
EEYOWOWOWOW
9-18 © 1980
McNaught Synd., Inc.
VET

"THAT WAS A COTTON SWAB...
...NOW FOR THE SHOT..."

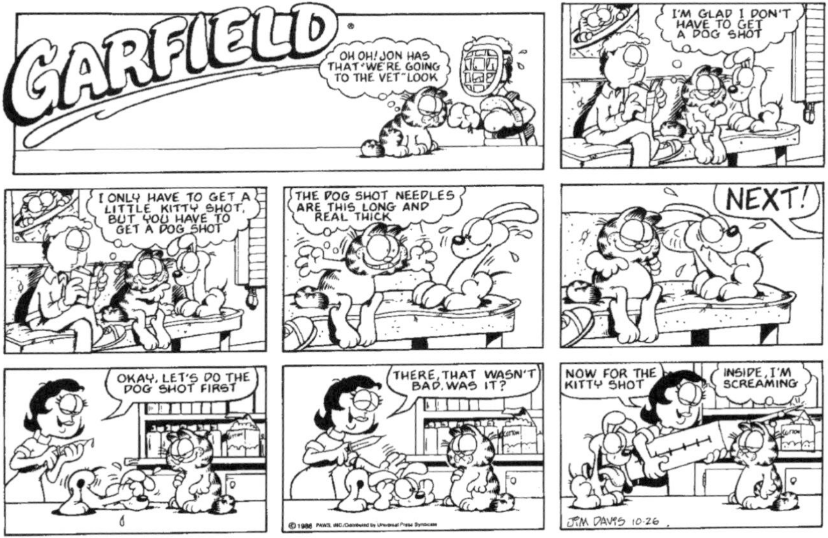
GARFIELD
OH OH! JON HAS THAT "WE'RE GOING TO THE VET" LOOK
I'M GLAD I DON'T HAVE TO GET A DOG SHOT
I ONLY HAVE TO GET A LITTLE KITTY SHOT, BUT YOU HAVE TO GET A DOG SHOT
THE DOG SHOT NEEDLES ARE THIS LONG AND REAL THICK
NEXT!
OKAY, LET'S DO THE DOG SHOT FIRST
THERE, THAT WASN'T BAD, WAS IT?
NOW FOR THE KITTY SHOT
INSIDE, I'M SCREAMING
JIM DAVIS 10-26

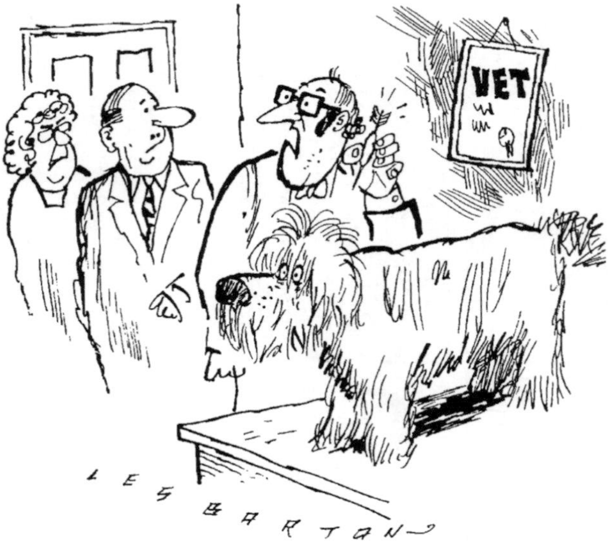
VET
LES BARTON

"I've discovered the reason for his migraine...this dart!"

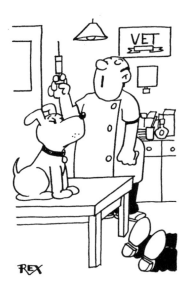

"There, now, that didn't hurt a bit, did it, boy?
O.K. Mr. Crudwell, you can take him home now."

For Better or For Worse® **by Lynn Johnston**

NO KIDDING! YOU PUT THE ELASTIC BAND AROUND HIS LEG! THEN THAT BIG CUT WAS YOUR FAULT!
I'M SORRY! I WAS JUST FOOLING AROUND, AN' I FORGOT IT WAS THERE!
I BET HE HATES ME!
© 1989 Universal Press Syndicate
NO HE DOESN'T, ELIZABETH. DOGS AREN'T LIKE THAT. A DOG IS ALWAYS WILLING TO GIVE HIS MASTER ANOTHER CHANCE.
5-13
REMEMBER... TO ERR IS HUMAN; TO FORGIVE CANINE!
GROAN.
Lynn

Specialty Vets

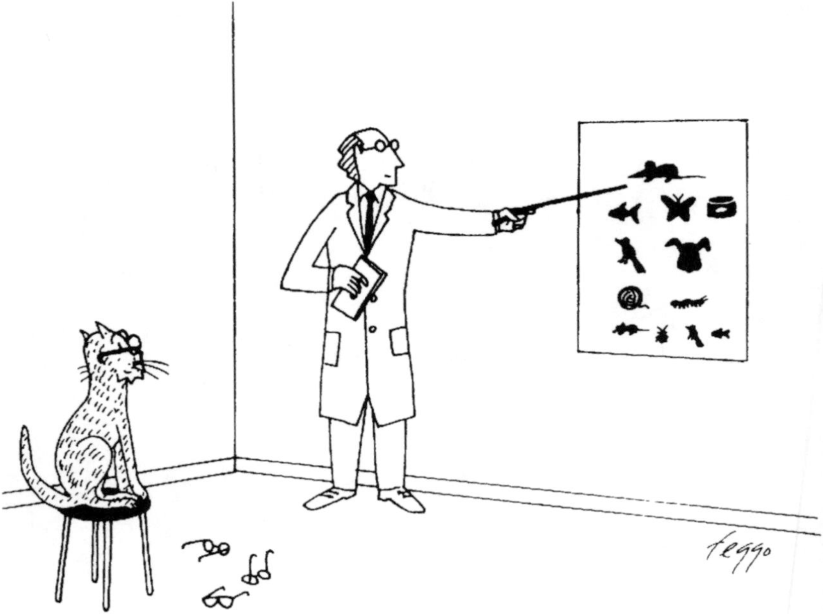
feggo

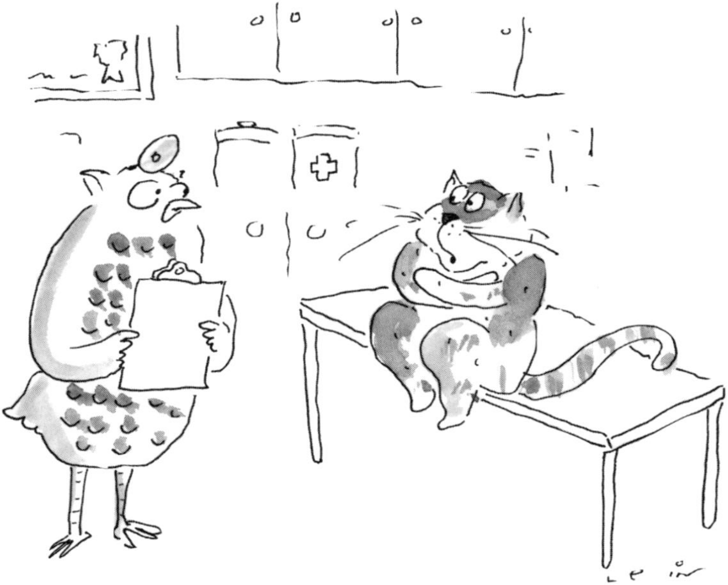

"I'm used to having a pussycat doctor."

Mother Goose & Grimm

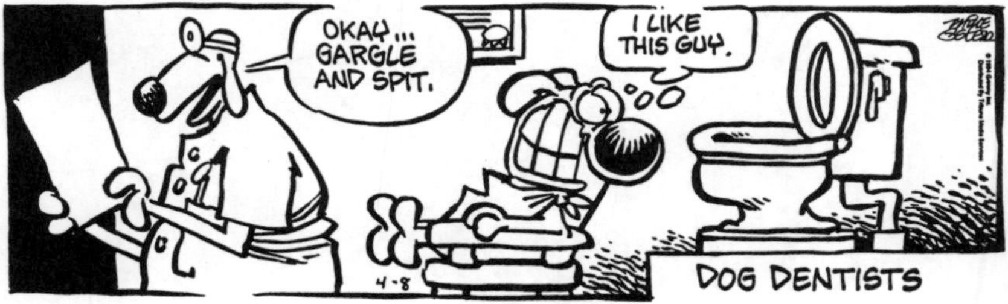
OKAY... GARGLE AND SPIT.
I LIKE THIS GUY.
4-8
DOG DENTISTS

WILLIAMS, M.
Chesire
ENGLAND

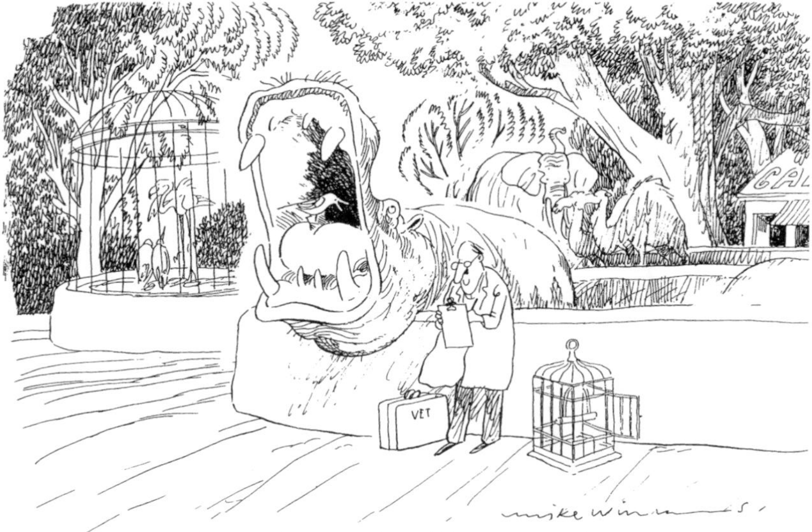
VET

"...upper right seven buccal filling....upper right six mesial filling with palatal extension..."

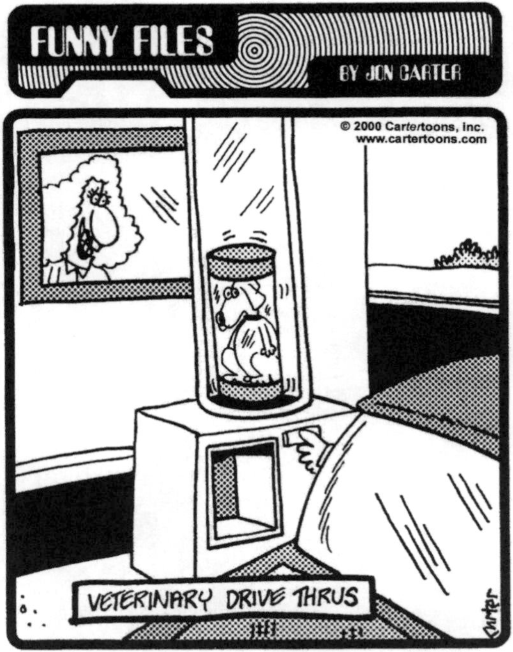
FUNNY FILES
BY JON CARTER
© 2000 Cartertoons, inc.
www.cartertoons.com
VETERINARY DRIVE THRUS
Carter

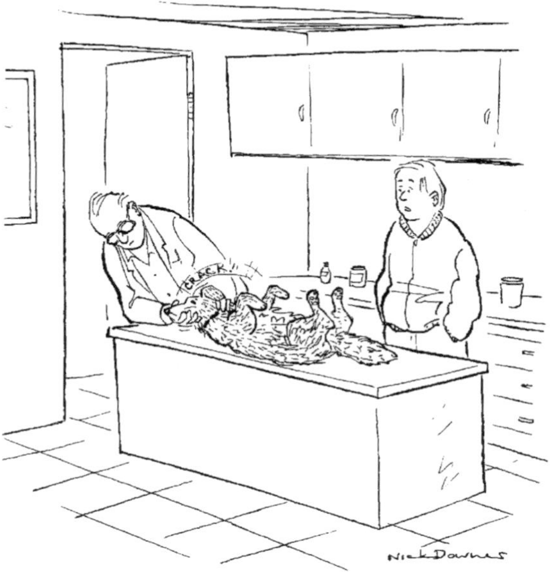
CRACK
Nick Downes

"Are there many veterinary chiropractors?"

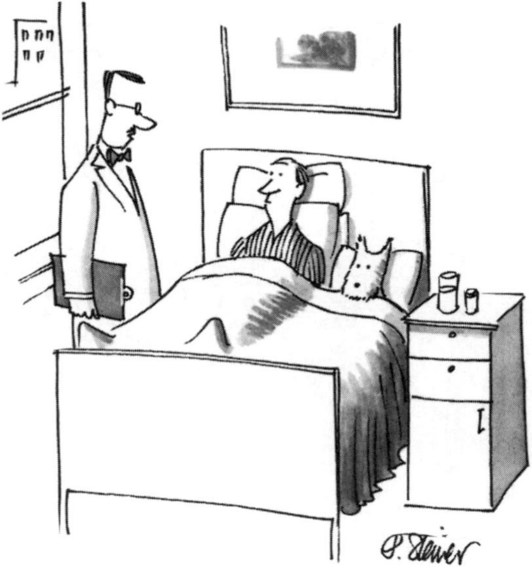
P. Steiner

"Under our holistic approach, Mr. Wyndot, we not only treat your symptoms, we also treat your dog."

Off the Couch

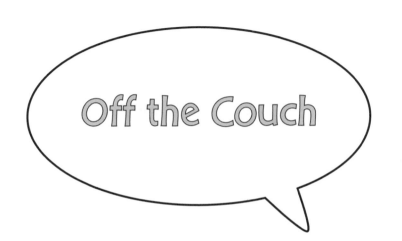

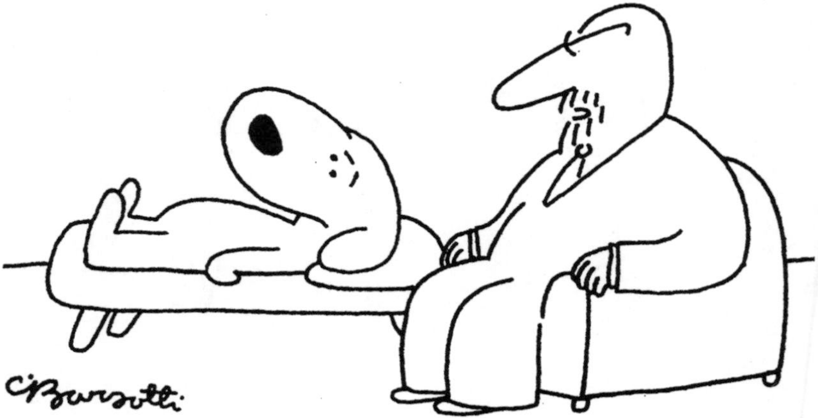
C Barsotti

"And only you can hear this whistle?"

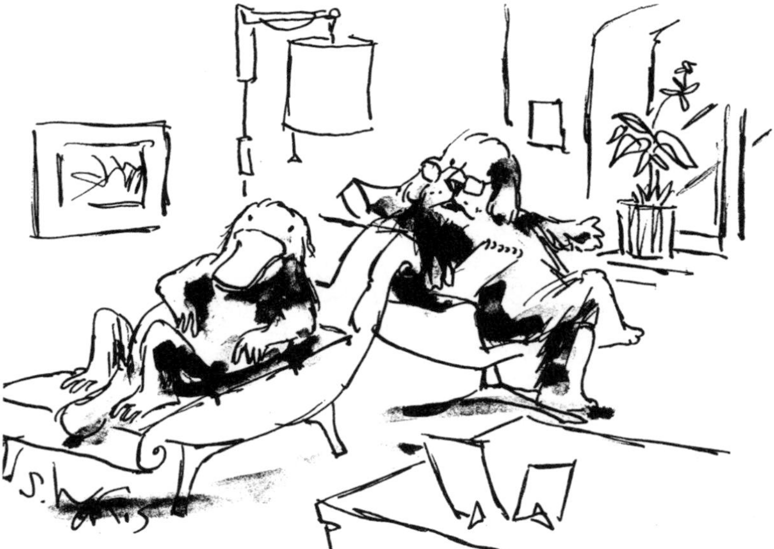

"YOU SHOULDN'T WORRY. ASIDE FROM THE DUCK BILL AND THE EGGS YOU'RE A PERFECTLY NORMAL MAMMAL."

FREE-ASSOCIATING

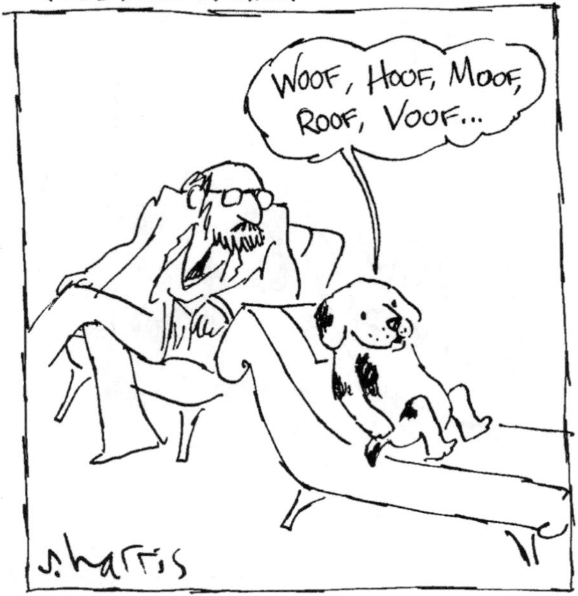

off the mark by Mark Parisi
www.offthemark.com
I HAVE A CONFESSION TO MAKE... I DON'T COME HERE TO BE PSYCHOANALYZED. I COME HERE 'CAUSE YOU LET ME ON THE COUCH...
ATLANTIC FEATURE
© 1994 MARK PARISI
www.offthemark.com
MARK PARISI

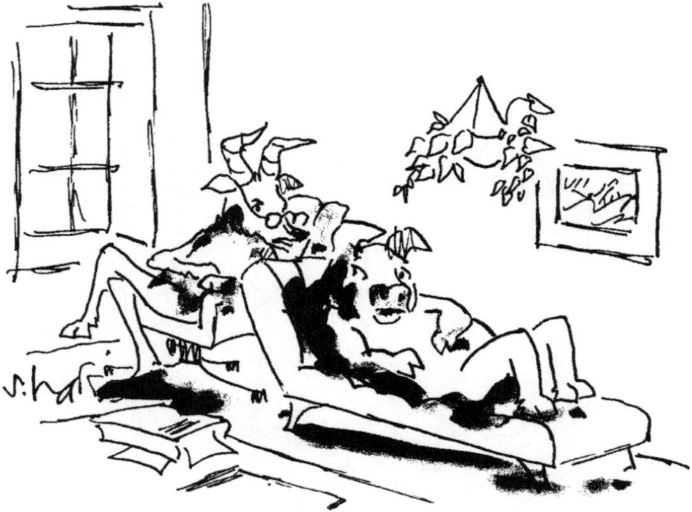

s. harris

"BELIEVE ME, FOR A PIG, HAVING TO LIVE IN A HOUSE OF STRAW IS NOT THE WORST THING THAT CAN HAPPEN TO YOU."

RICHTER
USA

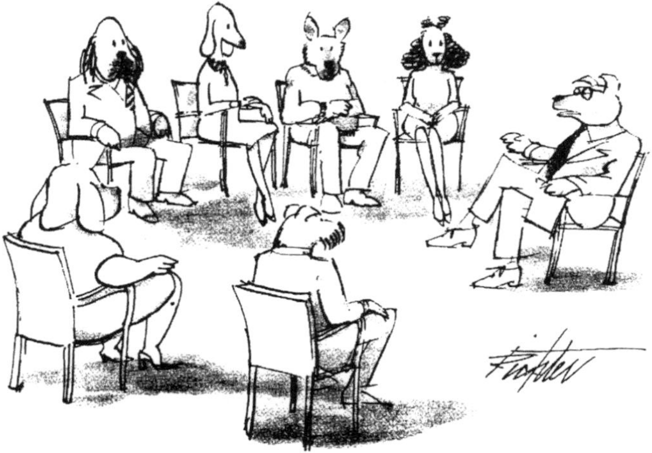
Richter

"O.k., who else has experienced the best friend relationship as inadequate?"

Side Effects

Strange Breed by Steve Langille
http://www2.hi.net/s4/strangebreed.htm

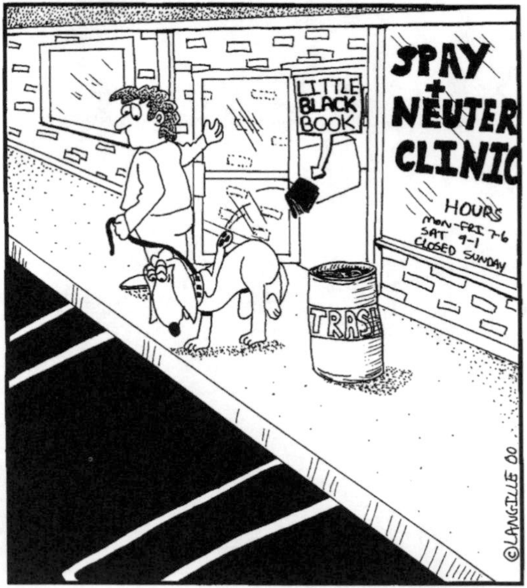
LITTLE BLACK BOOK
SPAY + NEUTER CLINIC
HOURS
MON-FRI 7-6
SAT 9-1
CLOSED SUNDAY
TRASH
©LANGILLE 00

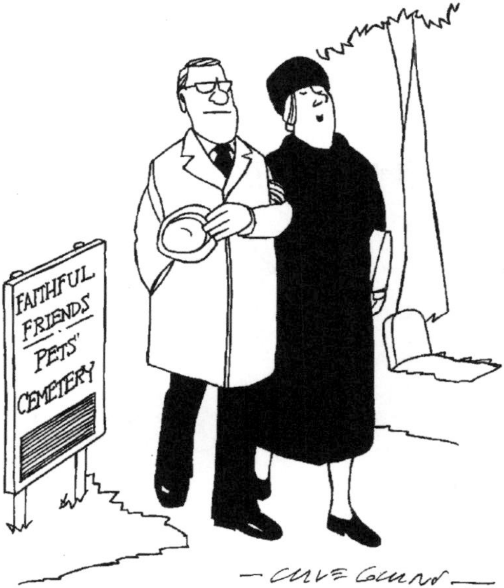
FAITHFUL
FRIENDS
PETS'
CEMETERY

"That was a nice touch–having
the vet buried with him."

off the mark by Mark Parisi
www.offthemark.com
EASY, SPARKY... JUST STAY CALM ... NOW, LET FLUFFY GO AND MAYBE WE'LL CALL OFF THIS NEUTERING THING, OKAY?
©1992 MARK PARISI
www.offthemark.com
MARK PARISI

Mutts

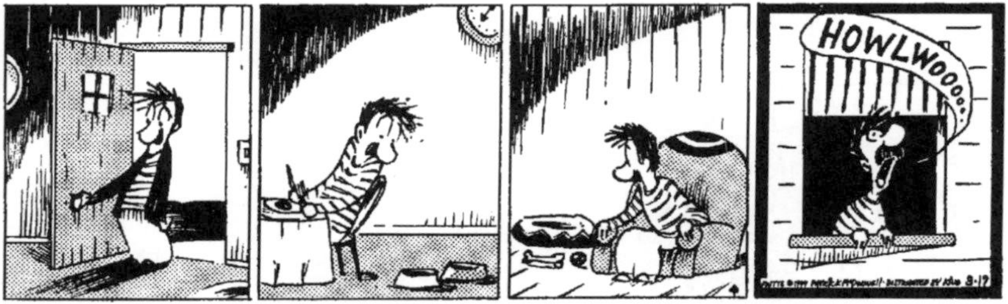
HOWLWOOOO...

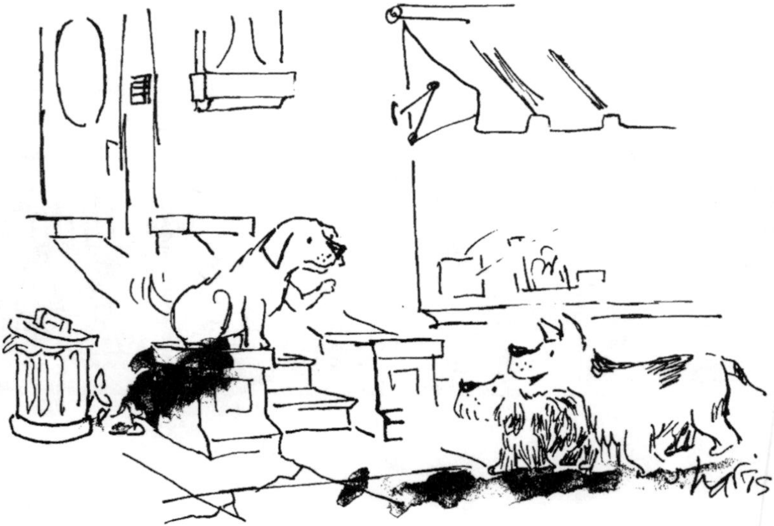

"SINCE I'VE BEEN NEUTERED I HAVE A LOT MORE PLATONIC FRIENDS THAN I USED TO HAVE."

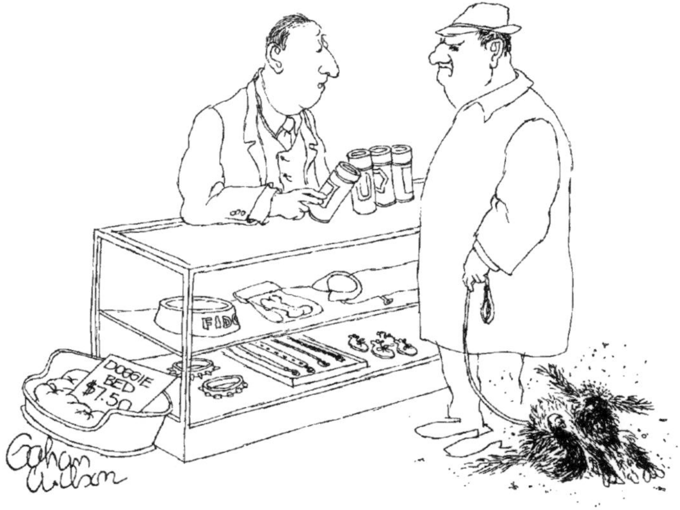
FIDO
DOGGIE
BED
$7.50

"This preparation will eliminate fleas, this one ticks, this one various other vermin and considerable fungi, and this one will eliminate the dog itself."

CHARLIE
SAVOY
PET HEADSTONES
office
IMMEDIATE DELIVERY ON SOME STONES!
BROWNIE
KING
BLACKIE
FLUFFY
SHEP
SPOT
© 1988 Tribune Media Services, Inc. All Rights Reserved
8-6

Mother Goose & Grimm

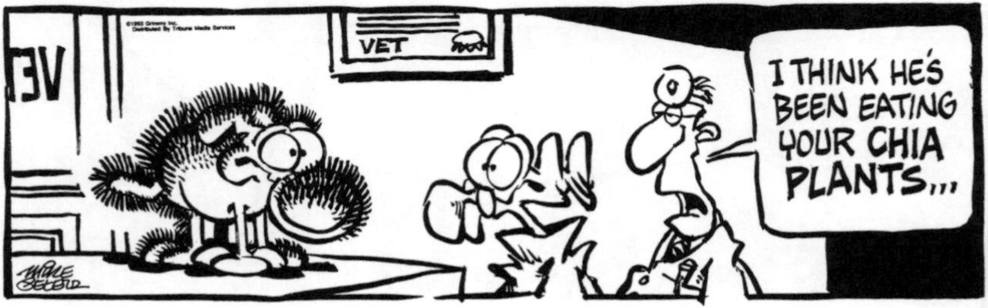

VET
I THINK HE'S BEEN EATING YOUR CHIA PLANTS...

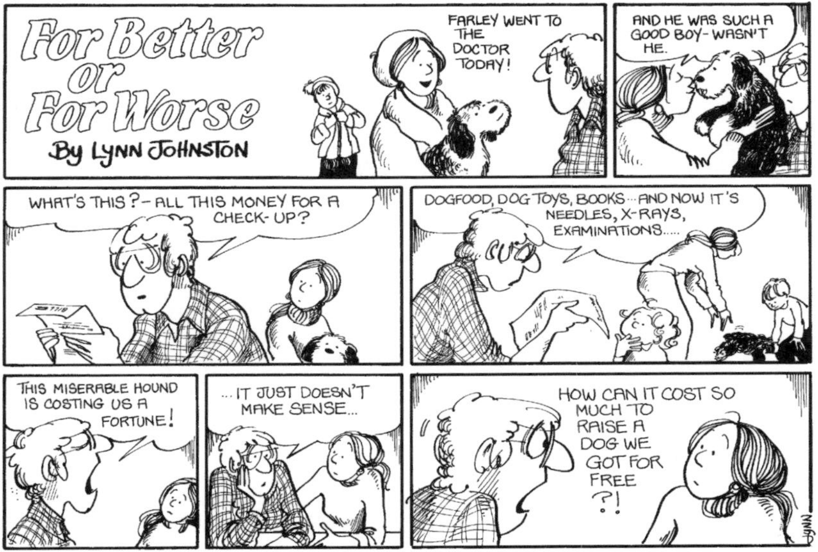
For Better or For Worse
By Lynn Johnston
FARLEY WENT TO THE DOCTOR TODAY!
AND HE WAS SUCH A GOOD BOY- WASN'T HE.
WHAT'S THIS?- ALL THIS MONEY FOR A CHECK-UP?
DOGFOOD, DOG TOYS, BOOKS... AND NOW IT'S NEEDLES, X-RAYS, EXAMINATIONS.....
THIS MISERABLE HOUND IS COSTING US A FORTUNE!
...IT JUST DOESN'T MAKE SENSE...
HOW CAN IT COST SO MUCH TO RAISE A DOG WE GOT FOR FREE ?!
LYNN

For Better or For Worse by Lynn Johnston

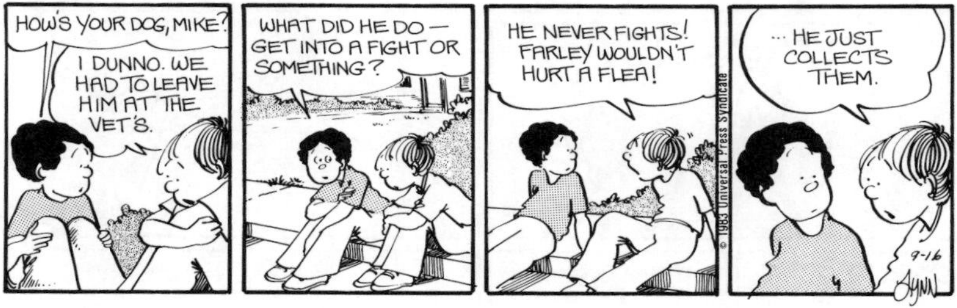
HOW'S YOUR DOG, MIKE?
I DUNNO. WE HAD TO LEAVE HIM AT THE VET'S.
WHAT DID HE DO — GET INTO A FIGHT OR SOMETHING?
HE NEVER FIGHTS! FARLEY WOULDN'T HURT A FLEA!
© 1983 Universal Press Syndicate
... HE JUST COLLECTS THEM.
9-16
LYNN

For Better or For Worse by Lynn Johnston

DON'T WORRY, MICHAEL. I'M SURE FARLEY WILL BE JUST FINE.
CAN I SAY SOME PRAYERS FOR HIM?
THAT WOULD BE A NICE IDEA.
© 1983 Universal Press Syndicate
CAN I GO DIRECTLY TO GOD?—OR DO I ASK FOR SOMEONE IN THE PET DEPARTMENT?
9-17
Lynn

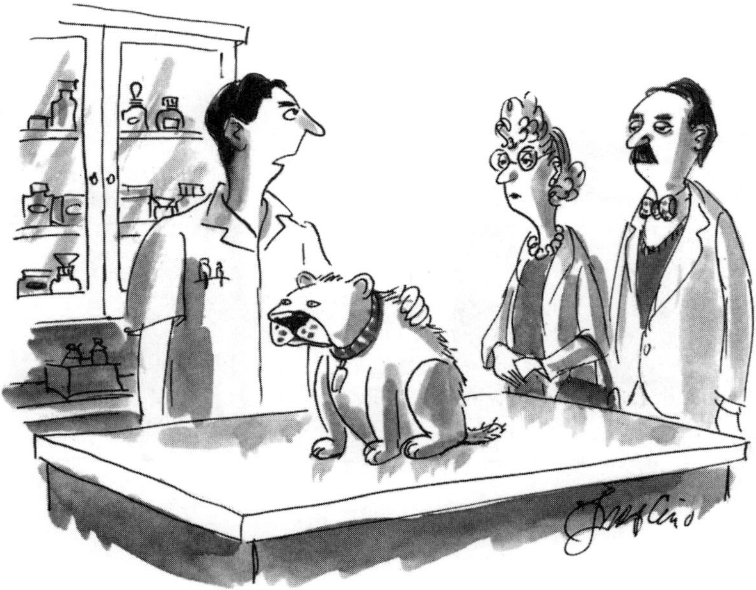

"He is physically able to wag his tail—given sufficient cause."

off the mark by Mark Parisi

www.offthemark.com

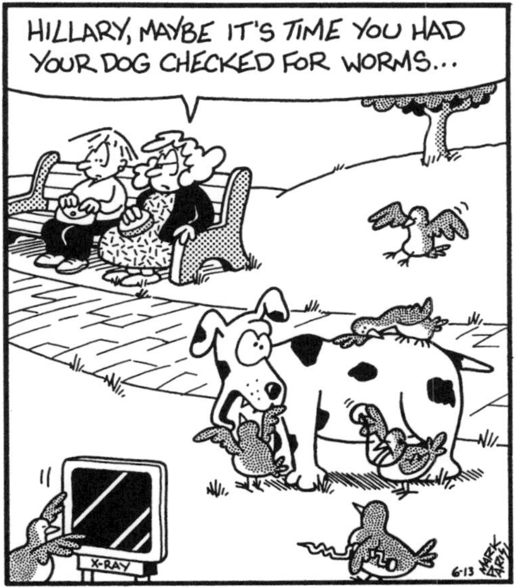
HILLARY, MAYBE IT'S TIME YOU HAD YOUR DOG CHECKED FOR WORMS...
X-RAY
6-13
MARK PARISI

For Better or For Worse® by Lynn Johnston

MOM, I DON'T THINK FARLEY HEARS VERY WELL.
I KNOW, HONEY.
I TOOK HIM TO THE VET LAST WEEK. THE DOCTOR TOLD ME THAT HE DOESN'T SEE TOO WELL NOW, EITHER.
1-29
FARLEY IS OVER 80 IN OUR YEARS. THESE THINGS HAPPEN WHEN YOU GET OLDER. - PETS ARE JUST LIKE PEOPLE!
© 1994 Lynn Johnston/Dist. by Universal Press Syndicate
...EXCEPT THAT THEY NEVER COMPLAIN!!
LYNN

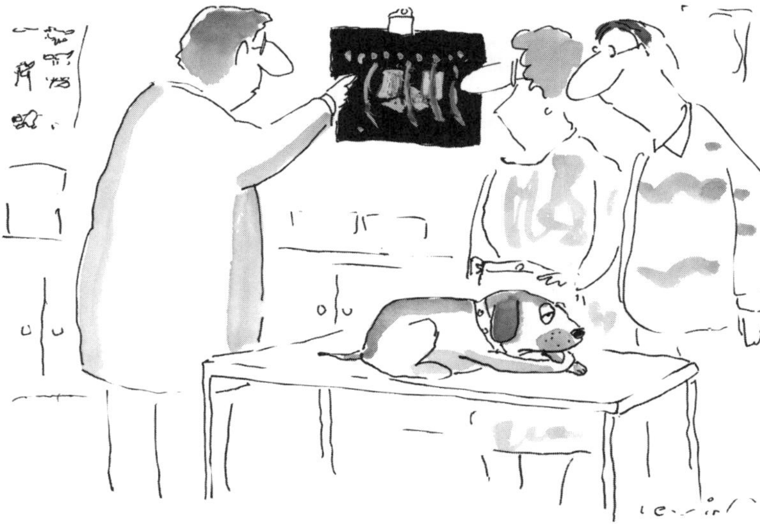

"He appears to have eaten some homework."

off the mark

by Mark Parisi

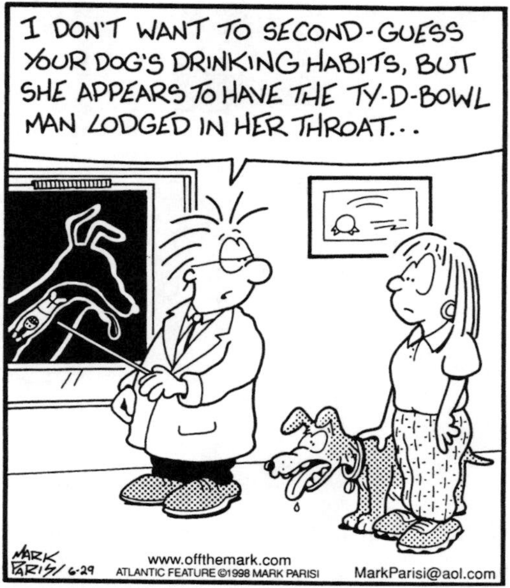
I DON'T WANT TO SECOND-GUESS YOUR DOG'S DRINKING HABITS, BUT SHE APPEARS TO HAVE THE TY-D-BOWL MAN LODGED IN HER THROAT...
MARK PARISI 6-29
www.offthemark.com
ATLANTIC FEATURE ©1998 MARK PARISI
MarkParisi@aol.com

Miscellaneous

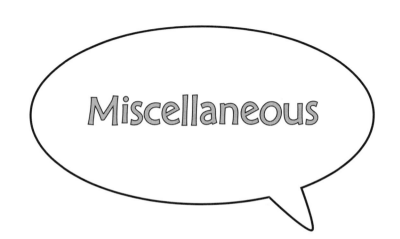

Mutts

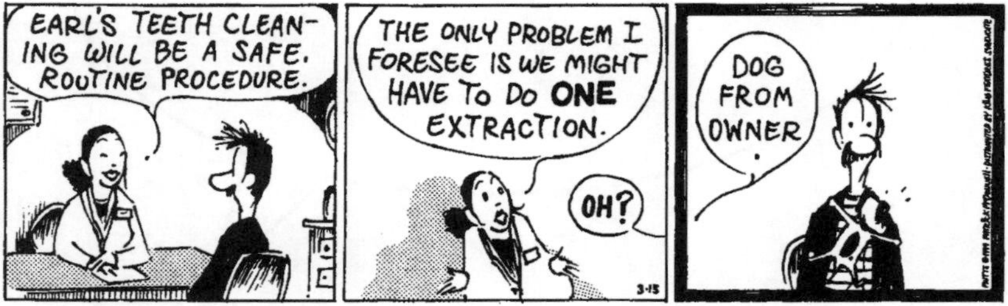
EARL'S TEETH CLEANING WILL BE A SAFE. ROUTINE PROCEDURE.
THE ONLY PROBLEM I FORESEE IS WE MIGHT HAVE TO DO **ONE** EXTRACTION.
OH?
3-15
DOG FROM OWNER

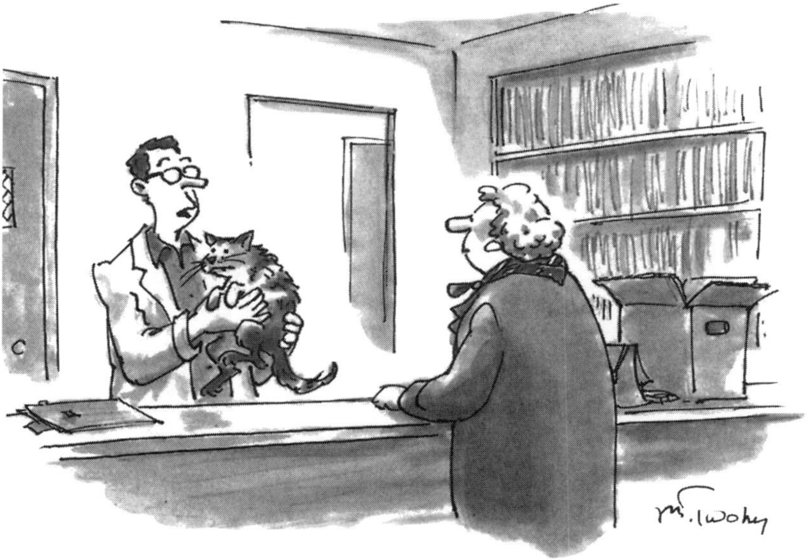

"I'm afraid we'll have to keep him overnight. Are you going to need a loaner?"

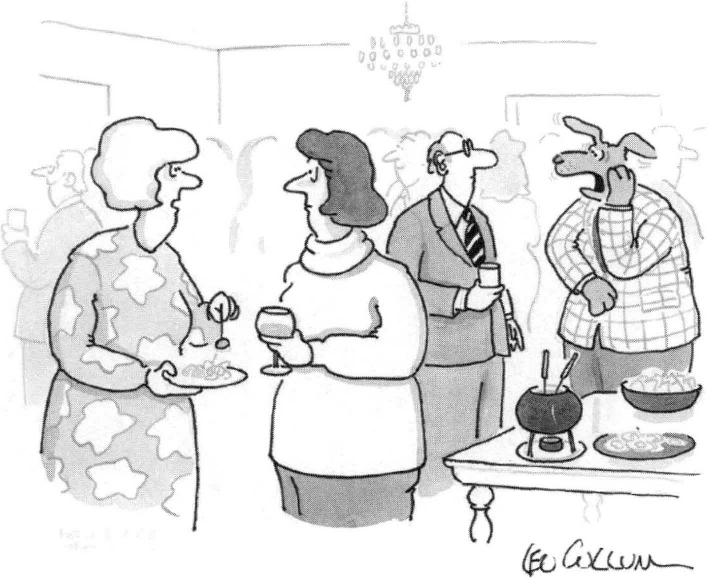

"As a veterinarian, Martin can't go anywhere without having someone ask for free advice."

Cornered by Baldwin

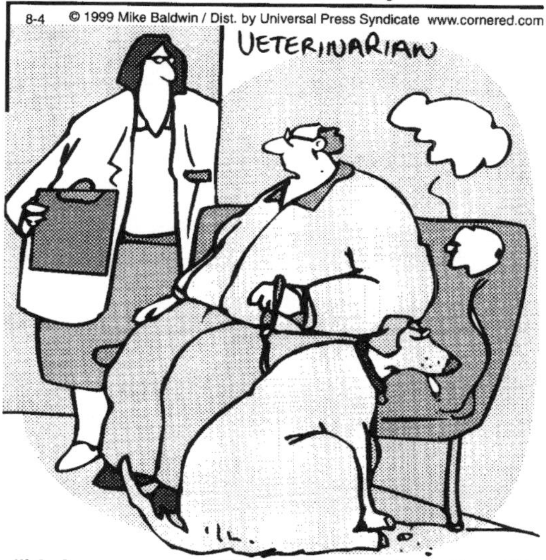
8-4 © 1999 Mike Baldwin / Dist. by Universal Press Syndicate www.cornered.com
VETERINARIAN

"He's nervous. Normally he'd wait until we got outside."

PEANUTS
SNOOPY'S AT THE VET'S?
YES, HE HAD TO STAY THERE OVERNIGHT FOR X-RAYS..
BUT THEY'LL KEEP HIM IN A CAGE OR SOMETHING, WON'T THEY? HOW WILL HE EVER STAND IT?
HERE'S THE WORLD WAR I FLYING ACE SITTING IN AN ENEMY PRISON CELL...

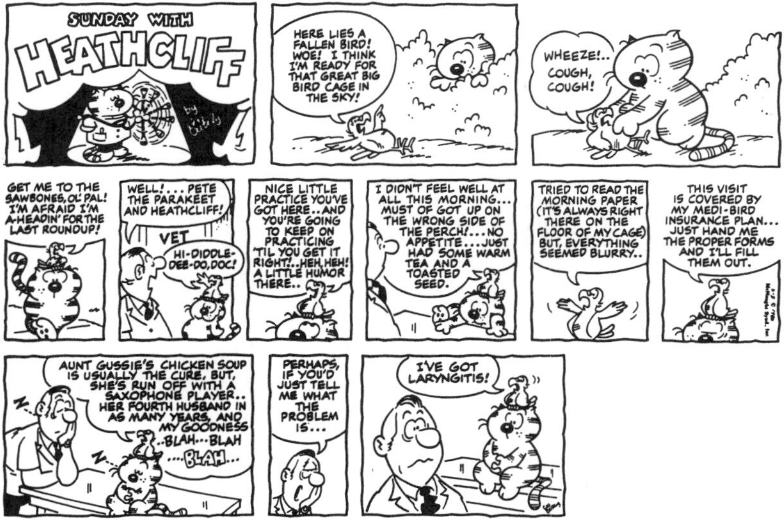
SUNDAY WITH
HEATHCLIFF
by Gately
HERE LIES A FALLEN BIRD! WOE! I THINK I'M READY FOR THAT GREAT BIG BIRD CAGE IN THE SKY!
WHEEZE!.. COUGH, COUGH!
GET ME TO THE SAWBONES, OL' PAL! I'M AFRAID I'M A-HEADIN' FOR THE LAST ROUNDUP!
WELL!... PETE THE PARAKEET AND HEATHCLIFF!
VET
HI-DIDDLE-DEE-DO, DOC!
NICE LITTLE PRACTICE YOU'VE GOT HERE.. AND YOU'RE GOING TO KEEP ON PRACTICING 'TIL YOU GET IT RIGHT!..HEH HEH! A LITTLE HUMOR THERE..
I DIDN'T FEEL WELL AT ALL THIS MORNING... MUST OF GOT UP ON THE WRONG SIDE OF THE PERCH!... NO APPETITE... JUST HAD SOME WARM TEA AND A TOASTED SEED.
TRIED TO READ THE MORNING PAPER (IT'S ALWAYS RIGHT THERE ON THE FLOOR OF MY CAGE) BUT, EVERYTHING SEEMED BLURRY..
THIS VISIT IS COVERED BY MY MEDI-BIRD INSURANCE PLAN... JUST HAND ME THE PROPER FORMS AND I'LL FILL THEM OUT.
AUNT GUSSIE'S CHICKEN SOUP IS USUALLY THE CURE, BUT, SHE'S RUN OFF WITH A SAXOPHONE PLAYER.. HER FOURTH HUSBAND IN AS MANY YEARS, AND MY GOODNESS ..BLAH...BLAH ....BLAH...
PERHAPS, IF YOU'D JUST TELL ME WHAT THE PROBLEM IS...
I'VE GOT LARYNGITIS!

Mutts

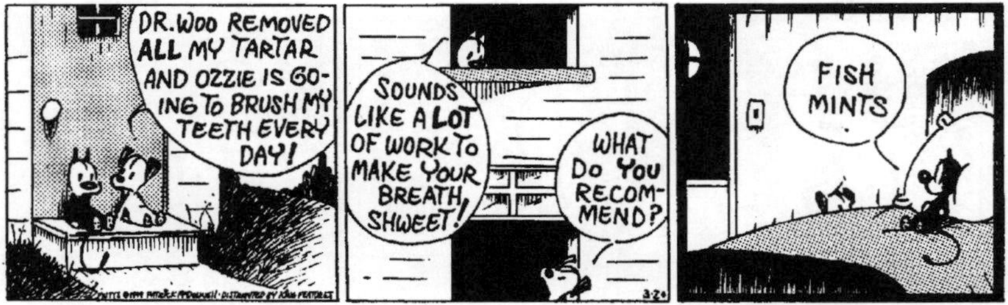
DR. WOO REMOVED ALL MY TARTAR AND OZZIE IS GO-ING TO BRUSH MY TEETH EVERY DAY!
SOUNDS LIKE A LOT OF WORK TO MAKE YOUR BREATH SHWEET!
WHAT DO YOU RECOM-MEND?
FISH MINTS

Mother Goose & Grimm

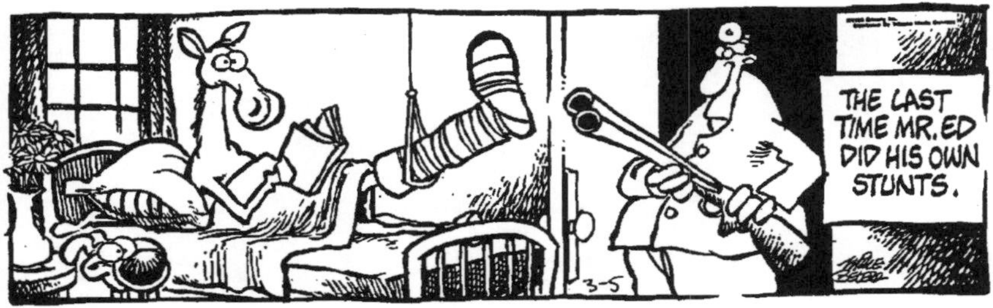
THE LAST TIME MR. ED DID HIS OWN STUNTS.
3-5

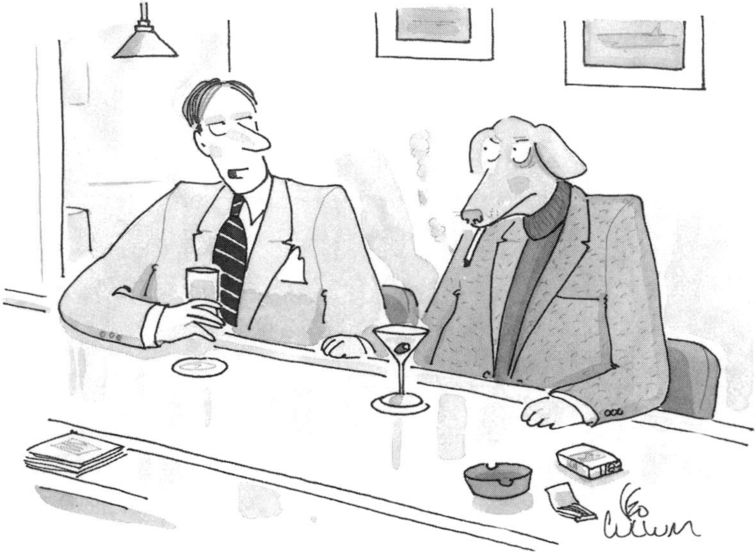

"Listen to me, Dave. I'm not just your friend, I'm your veterinarian."

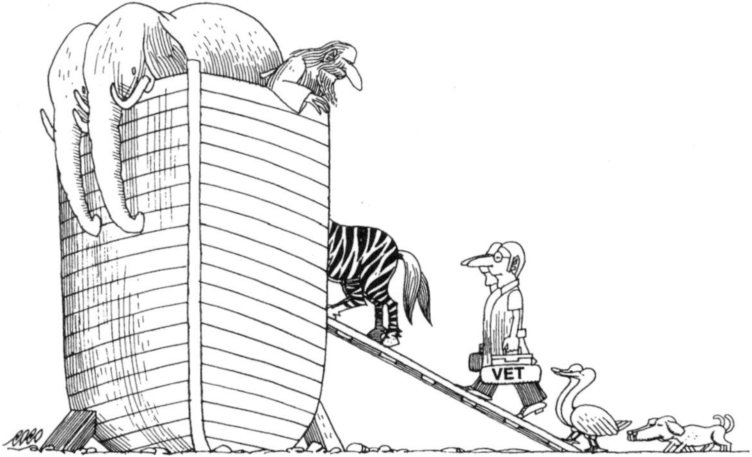
VET

Credits

Front cover

© 2000 Leo Cullum from cartoonbank.com. All Rights Reserved.

Take Me to Your Vet

GARFIELD © Paws, Inc. Reprinted with permission of UNIVERSAL PRESS SYNDICATE. All rights reserved.
© Werner Wejp-Olsen
© Tribune Media Services, Inc. All Rights Reserved. Reprinted with permission.
"Reprinted with special permission King Features Syndicate."
GARFIELD © Paws, Inc. Reprinted with permission of UNIVERSAL PRESS SYNDICATE. All rights reserved.
© Tribune Media Services, Inc. All Rights Reserved. Reprinted with permission.
ROBOTMAN reprinted by permission of Newspaper Enterprise Association, Inc.
ROBOTMAN reprinted by permission of Newspaper Enterprise Association, Inc.
ROBOTMAN reprinted by permission of Newspaper Enterprise Association, Inc.
REALITY CHECK reprinted by permission of United Feature Syndicate, Inc.
Nick Downes/(USA), CARTOONISTS & WRITERS SYNDICATE, www.cartoonweb.com

Waiting Room

© The New Yorker Collection 1993 Michael Crawford from cartoonbank.com. All Rights Reserved.
Reprinted with the permission of Simon & Schuster from I PAINT WHAT I SEE by Gahan Wilson. Copyright © 1971 by Gahan Wilson
CITIZEN DOG © 1999 Mark O'Hare. Dist. by UNIVERSAL PRESS SYNDICATE. Reprinted with permission. All rights reserved.
CITIZEN DOG © 1999 Mark O'Hare. Dist. by UNIVERSAL PRESS SYNDICATE. Reprinted with permission. All rights reserved.
CORNERED © Mike Baldwin. Reprinted with permission of UNIVERSAL PRESS SYNDICATE. All rights reserved.
GARFIELD © Paws, Inc. Reprinted with permission of UNIVERSAL PRESS SYNDICATE. All rights reserved.
© 2000 by Sidney Harris

Examination Room

© The New Yorker Collection 1992 Leo Cullum from cartoonbank.com. All Rights Reserved.
© Tribune Media Services, Inc. All Rights Reserved. Reprinted with permission.
CITIZEN DOG © 1999 Mark O'Hare. Dist. by UNIVERSAL PRESS SYNDICATE. Reprinted with permission. All rights reserved.
GARFIELD © Paws, Inc. Reprinted with permission of UNIVERSAL PRESS SYNDICATE. All rights reserved.
Reprinted by permission by ATLANTIC FEATURE SYNDICATE © MARK PARISI. All rights reserved.
© The New Yorker Collection 1997 Danny Shanahan from cartoonbank.com. All Rights Reserved.
© Tribune Media Services, Inc. All Rights Reserved. Reprinted with permission.
© The New Yorker Collection 1994 Mike Twohy from cartoonbank.com. All Rights Reserved.
"Herman® is reprinted with permission from LaughingStock Licensing Inc., Ottawa, Canada. All rights reserved."
CITIZEN DOG © 1999 Mark O'Hare. Dist. by UNIVERSAL PRESS SYNDICATE. Reprinted with permission. All rights reserved.
© Tribune Media Services, Inc. All Rights Reserved. Reprinted with permission.

Say Meow

Reprinted by permission by ATLANTIC FEATURE SYNDICATE © MARK PARISI. All rights reserved.
© Nicole Hollander
© Tribune Media Services, Inc. All Rights Reserved. Reprinted with permission.
BIZARRO © by Dan Piraro. Reprinted with permission of UNIVERSAL PRESS SYNDICATE. All rights reserved.
"By permission of George Gately and Creators Syndicate, Inc."
P.C. Vey/(USA), CARTOONISTS & WRITERS SYNDICATE, www.cartoonweb.com
© Tribune Media Services, Inc. All Rights Reserved. Reprinted with permission.
Reprinted by permission by ATLANTIC FEATURE SYNDICATE © MARK PARISI. All rights reserved.
"By permission of George Gately and Creators Syndicate, Inc."
"By permission of George Gately and Creators Syndicate, Inc."
ROSE IS ROSE reprinted by permission of United Feature Syndicate, Inc.
© Nicole Hollander
George Abbott/(USA), CARTOONISTS & WRITERS SYNDICATE, www.cartoonweb.com
"By permission of George Gately and Creators Syndicate, Inc."
"By permission of George Gately and Creators Syndicate, Inc."

Reprinted by permission by ATLANTIC FEATURE SYNDICATE © MARK PARISI. All rights reserved.
© Tribune Media Services, Inc. All Rights Reserved. Reprinted with permission.

There, There, That Didn't Hurt!

"By permission of George Gately and Creators Syndicate, Inc."
GARFIELD © Paws, Inc. Reprinted with permission of UNIVERSAL PRESS SYNDICATE. All rights reserved.
Les Barton/(England), CARTOONISTS & WRITERS SYNDICATE, www.cartoonweb.com
© www.cartoonstock.com
© Lynn Johnston Productions, Inc. / Distributed by United Feature Syndicate, Inc.

Specialty Vets

Felipe Galindo (Feggo)/(Mexico), CARTOONISTS & WRITERS SYNDICATE, www.cartoonweb.com
© The New Yorker Collection 1999 Arnie Levin from cartoonbank.com. All Rights Reserved.
© Tribune Media Services, Inc. All Rights Reserved. Reprinted with permission.
Mike Williams/(England), CARTOONISTS & WRITERS SYNDICATE, www.cartoonweb.com
© 2000 cartertoons, inc.
Nick Downes/(USA), CARTOONISTS & WRITERS SYNDICATE, www.cartoonweb.com
© The New Yorker Collection 1991 Peter Steiner from cartoonbank.com. All Rights Reserved.

Off the Couch

Copyright C. Barsotti
© 2000 by Sidney Harris
© 2000 by Sidney Harris
Reprinted by permission by ATLANTIC FEATURE SYNDICATE © MARK PARISI. All rights reserved.
© 2000 by Sidney Harris
Mischa Richter/(USA), CARTOONISTS & WRITERS SYNDICATE, www.cartoonweb.com

Side Effects

"Strange Breed" by Steve Langille. Slang46188@aol.com http://www2.hi.net/s4/strangebreed.htm
Clive Collins/(England), CARTOONISTS & WRITERS SYNDICATE, www.cartoonweb.com
Reprinted by permission by ATLANTIC FEATURE SYNDICATE © MARK PARISI. All rights reserved.

The Dog Ate My Homework

Miscellaneous

Back cover